Treatment Strategies for Abused Adolescents

Interpersonal Violence:
The Practice Series

Jon R. Conte, Series Editor

Interpersonal Violence: The Practice Series is devoted to mental health, social service, and allied professionals who confront daily the problem of interpersonal violence. It is hoped that the knowledge, professional experience, and high standards of practice offered by the authors of these volumes may lead to the end of interpersonal violence.

In this series...

Treatment Strategies for Abused Adolescents
From Victim to Survivor

Cheryl L. Karp
Traci L. Butler
Sage C. Bergstrom

Foreword by William N. Friedrich

Interpersonal Violence:
The Practice Series

SAGE Publications
International Educational and Professional Publisher
Thousand Oaks   London   New Delhi

For bulk purchases at reduced prices of *Activity Manual for Adolescents,* please contact the Sage Specials Sales Department nearest you.

SAGE Publications, Inc.
2455 Teller Road
Thousand Oaks, California 91320
E-mail: order@sagepub.com

SAGE Publications Ltd.
6 Bonhill Street
London EC2A 4PU
United Kingdom

SAGE Publications India Pvt. Ltd.
M-32 Market
Greater Kailash I
New Delhi 110 048 India

For information:

 SAGE Publications, Inc.
2455 Teller Road
Thousand Oaks, California 91320
E-mail: order@sagepub.com

SAGE Publications Ltd.
6 Bonhill Street
London EC2A 4PU
United Kingdom

SAGE Publications India Pvt. Ltd.
M-32 Market
Greater Kailash I
New Delhi 110 048 India

Printed in the United States of America

Library of Congress Cataloging-in-Publication Data

Karp, Cheryl L.
    Treatment strategies for abused adolescents : from victim to survivor / by Cheryl L. Karp, Traci L. Butler, Sage C. Bergstrom.
        p.   cm. — (Interpersonal violence ; v. 19)
    Includes bibliographical references and index.
    ISBN 0-7619-0950-8 (cloth : acid-free paper). — ISBN
0-7619-0951-6 (pbk. : acid-free paper)
    1. Sexually abused teenagers—Mental health. 2. Sexually abused teenagers—Rehabilitation. 3. Psychotherapy. I. Butler, Traci L.
II. Bergstrom, Sage C. III. Title. IV. Series.
RJ507.S49K37 1997
616.85'83—dc21   97-21010

98 99 00 01 02 03 04 10 9 8 7 6 5 4 3 2 1

Acquiring Editor: C. Terry Hendrix
Editorial Assistant: Dale Mary Grenfell
Production Editor: Michele Lingre
Production Assistant: Denise Santoyo
Typesetter/Designer: Andrea D. Swanson
Indexer: Molly Hall

Contents

PHASE I: ESTABLISHING THERAPEUTIC RAPPORT

PHASE II: EXPLORATION OF TRAUMA

PHASE III: REPAIRING THE SENSE OF SELF

PHASE IV: BECOMING FUTURE ORIENTED

Foreword

Important developmental considerations need to guide the therapist's selection of treatment approaches for children and adolescents. Too often, treatment books work for one age, but cannot be expected to work for two. In reviewing this book I contrasted the strategies outlined herein with the strategies presented in Cheryl Karp's and Traci Butler's book "Treatment Strategies for Abused Children" (1996). I am pleased to say that I found numerous differences that reflect not only clinically intuitive thoughts regarding the need of adolescents, but also an appreciation of the developmental differences between these two groups.

The differences that I noticed bring to mind one of the most stimulating books I have read in the past two years. It is Robert Kegan's "In Over Our Heads" (1994). In his book, Kegan elucidates the cognitive transformations that occur from 13-18 and how these changes affect the parenting and teaching of teenagers. Therapy with adolescents needs to move these individuals from a concrete to an abstract level of cognitive development. For example, it is often very useful to provide children with examples of different feeling stages. This gives children some awareness that people can have many different feelings, that these feelings have names, and that different feelings are related to different situations. However, that is not sufficient for an adolescent, who not only lives in a more complex world, he or she is also more capable of abstraction. The adolescent needs to begin to learn how to generalize from the simple identification of feelings states to situations in the future that are predictably related to different affective reactions. After some discussion, a child can say that they feel sad when their friend moves away, even though they may act angry. The teenager is already thinking ahead to loss that is inherent in relationship's, and choosing whether and how to experience it.

Adolescence is also the first time in which insight starts to be useful. For example, in the intrapersonal world of the child, a discussion of inner states will not have a lasting effect. However, this is something that is critical to the adolescent.

Kegan (1994) states that helping professionals can aid the teenager in holding multiple points of view simultaneously and begin to integrate them. The facilitation of this will be directly related to the clinician being sensitive to how the adolescent needs to begin to move forward, e.g., exploring ambivalent feelings about parental authority.

The author's references to Kohut (1971) and his seminal work on development of the self, reflects a theorectical perspective that is quite pertinent to adolescence. Adolescence is a time when individuals move from a developing self-concept to the capacity for subjectivity and self-consciousness. Their references bring to mind another seminal paper, this one by David Elkind, on the return of egocentricity in the adolescent (Elkind, 1974). The accepted self-absorption of the very young child spirals upward to return in a new, but necessary type of egocentricity in adolescence. This is the self-absorption that keeps the teenager believing that no one else has had these feelings, or felt this deeply. While this can make for wonderfully sensitive and passionate teenagers, in the the short term it puts them at increased risk for self-harm.

I was also gratified to see a number of activities that focus on the body. The return to egocentricity cited above is oftentimes very body-focused. The teenager's body, and more particularly the teenager's perspective about other people's perspectives on his or her body, again becomes a basic consideration. Victimization is directly related to one's sense of body integrity (Marquardt & Friedrich, in press). Consequently, the examination of one's body image and eventually correcting these distorted perceptions is something that is of critical importance. It is also a process that can genuinely begin in adolescence, given the new capacity for insight and abstraction about the self.

Finally, despite the developmental sensitivity of the strategies outlined, good therapy again requires opportunities for support, reflections, and enactment. This occurs because of the teenagers's therapeutic relationship as well as the supportive context in which they live. Creating this type of environment is the true "stuff" of therapy.

WilliamN. Friedrich
Professor and Consultant
Mayo Clinic and Medical School

❏ **References**

Elkind, D. (1974). Egocentrism in children and adolescents. In *Children and adolescents*. New York: Oxford University Press.

Karp, C. L. & Butler, T. L. (1996). *Treatment strategies for abused children: From victim to survivor.* Thousand Oaks, CA: Sage.

Kohut, H. (1971). *The analysis of the self.* New York: International University's Press.

Kegan, R. (1994). *In over our heads: The mental demands of modern life.* Cambridge, Massachusetts: Harvard University Press.

Marquardt, R. & Friedrich, W. N. (in press). Body image and perception and its relationship to victimization in adolescence. *Journal of the American Academy of Child & Adolescent Psychiatry.*

.

Introduction and Theory

Therapists who have worked with abused adolescents know the struggles and frustrations of trying to help them emerge from their experiences of trauma to become healthy survivors. We experienced similar struggles and frustrations as we searched the libraries and bookstores for new ideas and references to help us in our work with abused adolescents.

Each of us works in a different setting: private practice, middle school, and a residential treatment facility. We discovered that although a variety of materials are available for adult survivors, there are limited resources available for teens. At this point, we decided that our book should be focused on treatment of all adolescents who suffer from the effects of trauma—defined for the purposes of this book as the psychological effects suffered from sexual, physical, and emotional abuse.

Interestingly, child abuse has only been recognized as a significant social problem in the last few decades. It is rather disheartening to find that the Society for the Prevention of Cruelty to Animals, founded in 1866, preceded the Society for the Prevention of Cruelty to Children by 8 years. By the end of the 19th century, there were child protective agencies in England, France, Germany, Italy, the United States, and most other civilized countries (Karp & Karp, 1989, with Suppl. 1996).

The Society for the Prevention of Cruelty to Children was instrumental in getting protective laws passed regarding the importation of young children for sexual mistreatment and "white slavery." More recently, the Mann Act and the Lindbergh Law have provided a path toward more humane treatment and protection of children (Karp & Karp, 1989, with Suppl. 1996).

Post-traumatic stress disorder (PTSD) was not even a recognized disorder until the third edition of the *Diagnostic and Statistical Manual of Mental Disorders* (*DSM-III*; American Psychiatric Association, 1980) and was first established due to research with Vietnam War veterans. However, it was not until the revised edition of the *DSM* (*DSM-III-R*; American Psychiatric Association, 1987, pp. 247-251) that special provisions were made for the diagnosis of PTSD in children. PTSD symptoms in children were further elaborated in the most recent (fourth) edition, *DSM-IV* (American Psychiatric Association, 1994).

The most recent report prepared by the National Center on Child Abuse Prevention Research (Wang & Daro, 1997) is quite disturbing. This report revealed that 3,126,000 children were reported to Child Protective Services (CPS) agencies as victims of child maltreatment in 1996. This figure is based on information collected from 39 states. Nationwide, the rate of children reported for child abuse or neglect increased 12% during the period of time from 1991 to 1996. Overall, the total number of reports nationwide has increased 45% since 1987. A significant percentage of these involve youth from 12 to 17 years of age.

Our purpose in creating this book is to provide adolescents who have been abused or neglected with a tangible, activity-oriented means to work through the various phases of recovery from the abuse they have suffered, much like that provided for abused children in our previous book (Karp & Butler, 1996) and adult survivors of child sexual abuse in in Bass and Davis's (1988) book. Also included in each chapter are actual case examples and a "walk-through" of just how the activities can be applied. It is our hope that the case studies will further facilitate use of the activities by the therapist.

This book is *not* intended to assess whether an adolescent has been abused. Therefore, the clinical interview rather than the forensic interview is used to address specific areas of concern for the purpose of conducting psychotherapy. This is an important distinction in the treatment of abused children or adolescents. When the goal is to assess whether a person was abused, the forensic interview is used as part of the investigative process (Coulborn-Faller & Corwin, 1995; Coulborn-Faller & Everson, 1996a, 1996b; Karp, 1996). We can only assume that an assessment has been completed and that victims of abuse will benefit from the strategies set forth in this book.

We have included an interview schedule, the Child Abuse Trauma Interview for Adolescents (CATI-Ad), that we devised to assess the extent of the teen's abuse history (see Appendix). This is similar to the Child Abuse Trauma Interview (CATI) included in *Treatment Strategies for Abused Children* (Karp & Butler, 1996). We have borrowed many ideas for both of these from Briere's Child Maltreatment Interview Schedule for adult survivors of child maltreatment (Briere, 1992).

Many excellent resources review assessment of children suspected of being maltreated (Achenbach, 1991; American Professional Society on the Abuse of Children [APSAC], 1990, 1995; Briere, 1989; Coulborn-Faller & Corwin, 1995; Finkelhor & Associates, 1986; Garbarino, Guttmann, & Seeley, 1986; Gil, 1991; Gil & Johnson, 1993; Helfer & Kempe, 1987; Karp & Karp, 1989, Supp. 1996; MacFarlane, Waterman, et al., 1986; Zaragoza, Graham, Hall, Hirschman, & Ben-Porath, 1995).

The first chapter of this book briefly reviews adolescent social and sexual development and how this is disrupted by trauma. With the focus in society shifting to "abnormal" behaviors of children, we are often asked, "What is normal?" In this chapter, we have included a review of normal sexual development and issues that emerge at this stage of development. We have also included "red flags" of abnormal sexual behaviors.

In working with both teenage boys and girls, we have found that they process material very differently, particularly in group settings. We have also found specific differences in the healing process between adolescents and younger children. Although these distinctions may seem obvious, it is important to identify them specifically so that one's approach can be tailored to individual needs.

This book will focus on group as well as individual therapy. Most adolescents tend to organize their life in terms of peer groups, but some teens isolate themselves and are more comfortable in individual therapy. As self-esteem improves, many can progress to group work.

It has been our experience that teenage girls tend to be more verbally voluble and dramatic while processing their issues in group. Therefore, we found it to be important to provide a high degree of structure for the group by setting clear goals and guidelines. Several reminders to stay on task may be indicated. Teenage boys, on the other hand, tend to respond to the need for structure in a more accepting manner. This difference is well illustrated in Tannen's (1991) book on gender differences in communication styles, *You Just Don't Understand.*

Boys have special or unique issues that need to be addressed concerning sexual abuse (Bolton, Morris, & MacEachron, 1989; Crowder, 1995; Friedrich, 1995). The feelings of helplessness that arise as a result of being victimized may very well be disturbingly incongruent with the cultural expectations of being "a man" that they have internalized. If the perpetrator was an older woman, the male adolescent may experience a conflict between seeing himself as a "victim" and seeing himself as having made a sexual score or conquest.

Phobias regarding homosexuality may emerge as a result of the victimization to either the male or female teen. However, males seem to be more sensitive to the stigma associated with this concept. The result of these fears may be posturing by the male teen in an effort to establish what he sees as an acceptable male identity. This may appear as macho behavior.

Female adolescents who have been sexually abused, on the other hand, are judged much more severely if they act out or explore their sexuality. They are often labeled as "whores" or "sluts" by themselves or others. Therefore, it is difficult for them to build a healthy sexual identity, whether heterosexual or homosexual.

As previously stated, in addition to gender differences, you need to be aware that the adolescent healing process is generally different from that of younger children. If the adolescent was traumatized at a younger age and has not dealt with it, he or she has had many more years of concealing the pain. In addition, the earlier the trauma occurred, the more primitive the defenses are and the more ingrained the trauma is in the concept of self. Therefore, the healing process may be more complex. Adolescents may unrealistically view themselves as now "in control," not recognizing the underlying damage. Thus, they may put up invisible walls designed to keep themselves safe. It can be difficult to break through this exterior.

Because we have each worked in an institutional setting in addition to current positions, we have experienced the challenges of designing a program that demands flexibility due to the constant influx of new teens. When doing group therapy, you will need to decide whether to have open or closed groups and whether to have open-ended or time-limited groups. Just as you think you are past the introductory, rapport-building phase of treatment, a new adolescent comes in, and issues of trust need to be reworked. This can truly test your resolve.

If the group therapist can work with a consistent membership, all the better. However, many of us work in environments where children come and go at varying times in their treatment. Some may stay with you for a year; others may perhaps be under your care for only a month (e.g., in residential treatment or in a group home). Each time a teen leaves group, peers may experience not only genuine sadness but feelings of abandonment related to their trauma. When newcomers join the group, they may be put through a "testing" period during which they are sternly reminded of the "confidentiality" rule. The "old" members, as a group, may get closer until they decide how much they will trust and accept the new person. This repeated process may complicate working through the first stage considerably; the more cohesive the group is in membership, the easier it will be to build trust and rapport (Hepworth & Larsen, 1993).

Of course, if possible, it is best to have closed, time-limited groups in which all the teens enter at the same time and progress through the stages together. When that is not possible, perhaps a few individual sessions with the new participant could assist in integrating him or her into the group process.

Individual work may or may not be preferred by the adolescent. In general, teens are much more responsive to their peer group than to adults and will listen to their feedback more openly. Being in a one-to-one situation with an adult may place them in a less powerful position than they are comfortable with, not only because they want a "grown-up" identity at this stage of their development but because they may be reminded of being dominated by an adult when they were abused. Despite these considerations, some teens are so reluctant to let peers know of their "embarrassing secrets" that they may actually prefer individual therapy over group therapy. The higher-functioning and less-defended teen may use both modalities equally well.

This book has been designed to work in a variety of settings. It can be used in open or closed settings and with male, female, or mixed-gender groups. An important issue to consider is whether to include reactive abusers in your group. This is really dependent on the individual teen and the therapist's clinical judgment. If the main issue of the reactive abuser is the victimization, then that teen will probably be appropriate for the group as long as the teen also acknowledges the inappropriate behavior and is remorseful. If the adolescent is primarily a perpetrator, then those issues need to be addressed before the victimization issues. Such an individual would not be appropriate in an abuse recovery group until his or her perpetrator issues were addressed.

❏ Trauma and Its Effects

What does the word *trauma* actually mean? According to Everstine and Everstine (1993), *trauma* comes from the Greek root *traumat-*, meaning "wound." *Trauma* is a medical term for any sudden injury or damage to an organism. Just as physical trauma can overwhelm the body's defenses and cause distress and chronic pain, psychological trauma may overwhelm the mind's defenses. If left untreated, trauma can cause potentially lasting emotional harm. Psychological trauma results from an unforeseen occurrence that is experienced forcefully and very personally.

Everstine and Everstine (1993) noted that we commonly think of the occurrence itself as the "trauma." However, trauma is the response, the reaction. When defenses such as denial, repression, and rationalization are overwhelmed, trauma occurs. The more intensely the person's defenses are overwhelmed, the greater the trauma. A person's reaction to a traumatic event is not an abnormality revealing itself. The person's coping mechanisms for dealing with this shock have been set into motion. Therefore, there may be many degrees of trauma, from mild to severe. Everstine and Everstine (1993) described trauma as shocks to the system, lacerations of the spirit, and soul damage.

On a physiological level, trauma is perceived as a threat. Herman (1992) stated that initially the sympathetic nervous system is aroused, causing an adrenaline surge. The person in danger goes into a state of "alert." His or her attention is now focused on the immediate situation as ordinary perceptions of pain, fatigue, and hunger are forgotten. Strong emotions such as fear and anger may be present. These adaptive reactions of arousal, feelings, and perception are normal, preparing the person who is in danger. Traumatic reactions begin to occur when neither "fight" nor "flight" is possible. These normal responses to danger, having lost their usefulness, may continue to persist in a distorted manner long after the actual danger has gone (Herman, 1992).

Herman stressed that untreated traumas, especially chronic ones, can create deep and long lasting impairments to emotion, cognition, memory, and arousal. In addition, the normal integrating functions of these capabilities may become blocked. Various symptoms may become disconnected from their original source. Avoidant patterns, once developed, can prove dangerously maladaptive. A "cocoon," once protecting the individual from further harm, can decrease the traumatized individual's ability to cope and therefore affect his or her self-esteem. In addition, traumatic amnesia can have serious effects, particularly on children who are in the process of integrating important cognitions about the self and the world (Waites, 1993). A hundred years ago, Janet carefully documented this kind of fragmentation (Herman, 1992).

In the late 19th century, Janet, Charcot, Breuer, and Freud were studying the causes of hysteria. Responses to traumatic events were

then viewed as symptoms of hysteria. Both Janet and Freud identified these symptoms as "disguised representations of intensely
distressing events which had been banished from memory" (Herman, 1992, p. 12). "The Aetiology of Hysteria," a collection of 18 case
studies published by Freud in 1896, stated Freud's belief that "at the
bottom of every case of hysteria there are one or more occurrences
of premature sexual experience" (quoted in Herman, 1992, p. 13).
Because of the radical social implications of this theory, Freud and
others (Janet continued to support these groundbreaking concepts
and was ignored by the medical establishment) were forced to
repudiate their original theories for a more socially and politically
palatable viewpoint. Hysterical symptoms came to be designated as
"neurosis" and then explained away by psychoanalytic theory as
unconscious conflicts originating in childhood. The relevance of the
traumatic event itself becomes lost when the alleged neurotic conflict becomes the focus of treatment (Herman, 1992).

❏ Contemporary Theories
and Models of Treatment

Finkelhor and Browne (1986) proposed a model of analyzing the
effects of trauma in terms of four trauma-causing factors that they
referred to as "traumagenic dynamics." Although the context was a
discussion of the effects of sexual abuse, they also identified the four
factors as generalized dynamics associated with other kinds of trauma.

The four traumagenic dynamics are traumatic sexualization, stigmatization, betrayal, and powerlessness. According to Finkelhor
and Browne (1986), "These dynamics, when present, alter the child's
cognitive and emotional orientation to the world, and create trauma
by distorting a child's self-concept, world view, and affective capaci-
ties" (pp. 180-181).

Our hope is that adolescents suffering from the effects of trauma
will find the activities provided in the accompanying activity book
a safe way to explore abusive experiences. The goal of this project is
to assist the teen in moving from being a *victim* of abuse to being a
healthier *survivor*. We believe this process is accomplished through

provision of "corrective" and "reparative" experiences, as Eliana Gil has described them in her book *The Healing Power of Play* (1991).

According to Gil (1991), a corrective approach provides experiences within a safe and trusting environment that enables the victim to gain a sense of safety and trust and an enhanced sense of self. The reparative aspect of treatment is designed to assist in processing the traumatic events, allowing the victim to understand and incorporate the experiences in a healthier manner.

Another important aspect of child abuse trauma is covered by Briere (1989, 1992) in his explanation of the "abuse dichotomy." Negative self-evaluation may arise from the victim's attempt to make sense of his or her abusive experiences. This process can eventually lead to the child's and, later, the adolescent's perceptions that he or she is inherently bad and therefore deserved the abuse.

According to Briere (1992), the series of quasi-logical inferences, characterized by the child's dichotomous thinking and egocentricity, appears to proceed as follows:

1. "I am being hurt, emotionally or physically, by a parent or other trusted adult.
2. Based on how I think about the world thus far, this injury can only be due to one of two things: Either I am bad or my parent is (the abuse dichotomy).
3. I have been taught by other adults, either at home or in school, that parents are always right, and always do things for your own good (any other alternative is very frightening). When they occasionally hurt you, it is for your own good, because you have been bad. This is called punishment.
4. Therefore, it must be my fault that I am being hurt, just as my parent says. This must be punishment. I must deserve this.
5. Therefore, I am bad as whatever is done to me (the punishment must fit the crime: anything else suggests parental badness, which I have rejected). I am bad because I have been hurt. I have been hurt because I am bad.
6. I am hurt quite often, and/or quite deeply, therefore I must be very bad." (p. 28)

The abuse dichotomy can lead to cognitive distortions that persist well into adulthood. As can easily be seen, this unhealthy thought process can lead to negative conclusions about one's self-worth.

Experts in the field of child maltreatment agree that cognitive distortions created by physical, sexual, and psychological abuse have devastating, lifelong effects if left untreated (Briere, 1992; Finkelhor & Browne, 1986; Gil, 1991).

DSM-IV (American Psychiatric Association, 1994) listed diagnostic criteria for PTSD, the diagnosis most closely associated with victims of interpersonal violence, such as torture, rape, physical assault, and child abuse. *DSM-IV* has been revised to include specific symptoms attributed to children who suffer from PTSD.

A diagnosis of PTSD is based on a fairly constant set of symptoms that includes intrusive thoughts, numbing, hyperarousal, and the avoidance of triggering events. In addition to post-traumatic stress symptoms, secondary reactions to traumatic events, such as depression, substance abuse, and personality disorders, may complicate arriving at a diagnosis of PTSD.

PTSD is almost never the only diagnosis given. Nearly 50% of PTSD victims also suffer from major depression. Some studies have shown that upwards of 80% of those diagnosed with borderline personality disorder have been abused as children (Kroll, 1993). Therefore, it is important to realize that PTSD is not the only diagnosis that will distinguish whether an adolescent has a history of abuse.

Most studies that examine post-traumatic stress in child abuse focus on sexual and physical abuse. When PTSD is associated with psychological abuse, children have generally been "terrorized" or have witnessed violent assaults on others (Briere, 1992; Terr, 1990).

The practice guidelines for evaluating psychological maltreatment that have been prepared by APSAC (1995) cover six forms of psychological maltreatment: (a) spurning, (b) terrorizing, (c) isolating, (d) exploiting/corrupting, (e) denying emotional responsiveness, and (f) unwarrantedly denying mental health care, medical care or education. According to the guidelines, a repeated pattern or an extreme incident of the above conditions constitutes psychological maltreatment. It conveys a message that the child is "worthless, flawed, unloved, endangered, or only valuable in meeting someone else's needs" (APSAC, 1995, p. 7).

In reviewing the effects of abuse, it is important to address various factors that result in an increase in trauma. Briere (1992) mentioned several studies addressing certain characteristics that are associated with greater trauma than abuse without such characteristics: greater duration and frequency of the abuse (Elliott & Briere, 1992); multiple perpetrators (Peters, 1988); presence of penetration or intercourse (Finkelhor, Hotaling, Lewis, & Smith, 1989); physically forced sexual contact (Fromuth, 1986); abuse at an earlier age (Zivney, Nash, & Hulsey, 1988); concurrent physical abuse (Briere & Runtz, 1989); and victim feelings of powerlessness, betrayal, and/or stigma at the time of the abuse (Henschel, Briere, Magallanes, & Smiljanich, 1990).

The above studies emphasize the need to address the impact of abuse from various perspectives. The adolescent victim has often suffered many of the abusive experiences that are listed above. It is not unusual that a victim who has been physically and sexually abused has also suffered psychological maltreatment. Many adolescents have been abused at a very young age by physical force and have been made to feel powerless and betrayed by the perpetrator.

In his recent book *Psychotherapy With Sexually Abused Boys* (1995), Friedrich proposed an integrated contextual model in the treatment of sexual abuse. He outlined three broad theoretical perspectives that emphasize (a) the phenomenon of *attachment* as a central component in children's development in response to stress, (b) the *disregulating* aspect of trauma, and (c) the effect of trauma on the child's *sense of self*. His integrated model subsumes the traumagenic factors, information-processing, and PTSD models of trauma, as well as providing an additional developmental and family context.

Friedrich's book is organized around his theory regarding the three large domains of attachment, dysregulation, and self. For each domain, he presents first an overview and then a chapter on individual therapy, group therapy, and family therapy strategies. The model presented by Friedrich is consistent with the model proposed in this book. Friedrich's book is well organized and well written, and although it focuses on abused boys, it can readily be applied to girls.

❑ Abuse-Focused Psychotherapy

We have used a framework based on abuse-focused psychotherapy to address all aspects of child maltreatment. As Briere stressed in *Child Abuse Trauma* (1992), the message conveyed to adult survivors of child maltreatment in abuse-focused psychotherapy is acknowledgment of the struggle to survive the child maltreatment. Further, coping behaviors that are often seen as sick or dysfunctional are reframed as healthy accommodations to the toxic environment.

Abuse-focused psychotherapy for adolescents, as for adults and children, is not about a cure but about survival. The individual's work is to gain the courage to go back to the frightening thoughts and images of the trauma and explore them in a safer environment where there is a better sense of control. The teen must then gain the skills necessary to cope with what he or she may see as a frightening world, even today, to be able to grow up as a healthier adult.

The therapist's job is to create a safe, nurturing, and protective setting in which the adolescent can do this important work. Unless the individual feels safe and protected, he or she will most likely not engage in this process of healing. Therefore, setting the stage for a healthy therapeutic bond is a necessary beginning of the healing process.

In approaching the adolescent victim of abuse, as in approaching the child victim, we have used an abuse-focused psychotherapy that is based on a phenomenological therapeutic stance and the premises of self psychology theory. Phenomenology is a theory that behavior is determined by the survivor's personal experiences and perceptions rather than reality as it can be described in physical, objective terms.

Self psychology, based on the theories offered by Kohut and colleagues (Elson, 1987; Kohut, 1971, 1977), focuses on the emergence of the self. Although the concept of the "self" has yet to be clearly defined (Briere, 1992; Stern, 1985), "the sense of self stands as an important subjective reality, a reliable, evident phenomenon that the sciences cannot dismiss. How we experience ourselves in relation to others provides a basic organizing perspective for all interpersonal events" (Stern, 1985, p. 6).

Briere (1992) noted that severe child maltreatment may interfere with the child's access to a sense of self. This creates a situation in which the child is prone to identity confusion, boundary issues, and feelings of personal emptiness. Self psychology theory stresses the importance of empathy and mastery in the formation of self-esteem. It is rooted deeply in child development.

In working with adolescent victims of maltreatment, we believe it is important to be empathic and child focused. One must address the victim's behaviors and feelings from his or her perspective to understand the meaning and impact of the abuse for him or her.

In some of the activities, we have used cognitive-behavioral techniques such as cognitive restructuring to assist the victim in challenging his or her distorted perceptions. These are important tools in the adolescent's struggle toward developing a healthier sense of self.

❏ Phases of the Recovery Process

There are four general phases of the recovery process. In the first phase, *establishing therapeutic rapport,* the therapist builds a positive therapeutic relationship by providing a safe and nurturing environment that encourages a sense of trust. Friedrich (1995) explored this stage in his section on attachment issues.

Chapters 2 through 4 focus on the first phase of recovery. The activities are designed to be less threatening and to encourage the adolescent to begin building therapeutic rapport, identifying feelings, and exploring boundaries without focusing specifically on the trauma.

It is important to note that traumatized individuals have an impaired ability to trust others and typically have difficulties with appropriate boundaries. Abused individuals often have impaired abilities to judge the trustworthiness of others. Some teens will have loose boundaries and give "blanket trust" (placing themselves in potentially unsafe situations), whereas others will not trust anyone.

Establishing trust and establishing appropriate boundaries are crucial aspects of trauma resolution. There is no set time for how long this process may take. We are mindful of the time constraints of a residential setting and managed care. In our opinion, trauma resolution is not typically conducive to short-term therapy. Therefore, if you are working within a managed-care setting, it will be unrealistic to expect the adolescent to complete his or her treatment within a brief period of time. You may be able to focus only on the first and possibly second phase of recovery before the allotted time is up. Regardless, it is important to go at a pace specific to the needs of each individual. If the first phase is not well established, there is potential to retraumatize the adolescent by moving into the reparative phase prematurely.

The second phase of recovery, *exploration of trauma*, entails the exploration of various aspects of the trauma. This phase incorporates both of Gil's goals of treatment, the corrective and the reparative experiences, and constitutes the abuse-focused aspect of treatment. It is covered in Chapters 5 through 7, which include activities identifying specific people and places that feel unsafe, as well as "secrets," memories, flashbacks, and nightmares associated with traumatic experiences. In the foreword of *Treatment Strategies for Abused Children* (Karp & Butler, 1996), Friedrich (1996) stated that the emphasis on disclosure of the trauma has direct relevance to the disregulating effect of unarticulated trauma covered in his "dysregulation" domain. This can be an extremely difficult and time-consuming process in therapy. As the trauma is being recalled, you may find yourself back at the beginning stages of therapy.

The foundation of trust may begin to crumble as specific aspects of the traumatic experience(s) are remembered, resulting in the projection of distrust onto you as the therapist (or other group members). For example, a therapist may tell the individual that they will have a "special relationship" in which it is safe to share secrets. This may be interpreted to be similar to the "special," "secret" relationship that was shared with the abuser. Such an interpretation can foster all sorts of fears undermining the foundation of trust that was previously built. In addition, many victims were told by the perpetrator that the perpetrator just "loved them too much." This "special" relationship can create confusion in the developing adolescent, who is going through a myriad of changes, including hormonal effects.

Another therapeutic consideration when dealing with teens is the gender of the therapist and of the victim. Although this may not be specific to recalled memories of abuse, it may interfere with the trust aspect of therapy. Because many preteens and teens are dealing with hormonal changes and are prone to "fall in love" with "idealized images" (e.g., their teachers, movie stars), special attention to the possibility of projected feelings toward the therapist may need to be addressed. In group therapy, a female and male cotherapist team may be more effective in working with teens who are in later stages of recovery and ready to address gender-specific issues with their perpetrators. If you note any distress among any of the group members, you will need to go back to safer, rapport-building activities. After addressing any issues of projection, you can then move on to the more challenging activities of the third phase of recovery.

The third phase, covered in Chapters 8 and 9, is *repairing the sense of self*. This includes processing various aspects associated with guilt and shame stemming from the trauma, working through "stuck" feelings, and developing such skills as assertiveness and problem solving to cope with ongoing feelings. Friedrich's (1995) "self" domain encompasses both the third and fourth phases outlined in this book.

Guilt and shame are often so entrenched in the individual's sense of self that it may be difficult to let go of these unhealthy beliefs completely. The activities in this book address this difficult phase of recovery, hopefully leading to a sense of mastery, increased control, and an ability to trust.

To us, guilt and shame are at the core of the damage done by abusive experiences, leading to seriously impaired self-esteem. Reparation of the self can become a lifelong process, even when various aspects of the trauma have been resolved. The activities outlined in this book are a powerful adjunct to your therapy work with abused adolescents. However, they are not meant to be the only means of therapy.

The final phase, as we see it, is assisting the adolescent in *becoming future oriented*. As the long journey of his or her own recovery is explored, it is important not only to look at the here and now and all of the accomplishments achieved thus far but to look toward the future. Chapter 10 is designed not only to review the accomplishments thus far but to assist in setting future goals.

Throughout the process of trauma resolution, the individual is so identified with the victim role that it can be difficult to move from the helplessness associated with abuse to a sense of healthy empowerment and control. Unfortunately, some victims use unhealthy means of gaining a sense of empowerment and control, such as perpetrating abuse against others. This will be covered in more detail in Chapter 1, which deals with developmental issues.

We strongly believe that it is critical to assist the adolescent in learning skills necessary to deal with the here and now as well as in setting goals for the future. It is hoped that the adolescent will emerge as a healthier survivor, rather than remaining a victim of his or her past.

❏ Therapist Issues

We have found through our own work with abused children and adolescents that you, as the therapist, will experience a myriad of feelings as you work through the abuse. You need to be aware of them and expect them.

When working with abused children and adolescents, it is best for therapists with abuse histories to have worked through their own traumas to a large degree. Periodically, it may be necessary for them to reenter their own therapy so that issues elicited by the abuse do not interfere with the adolescent's therapy.

You may feel personally overwhelmed as you walk through the pain with the victim while working through the phases of recovery. We have found that having a colleague to confide in and help us process through the emotional aspects of each case has enhanced our therapeutic effectiveness and has helped us to keep a healthier perspective.

Various warning signs may alert you to the possibility that therapeutic boundaries are an issue. You may find yourself feeling sorry for the victim and needing to rescue him or her from the abusive experiences. This is not establishing healthy boundaries.

You may also find yourself angry because you sense that your nurturing behaviors have been exploited. If this is the case, your relationship has become too enmeshed. Such an unhealthy relationship can manifest itself in various behaviors exhibited by the teen, from demanding constant attention, to venting anger at you with assaultive actions, to attempting to manipulate you.

The psychodynamic concept of transference is applicable when working with abuse victims. The individual transfers the thoughts and feelings about a primary person in his or her life onto a safer person, the therapist. The therapist may then react to the victim's behavior in a countertransference, often resulting in hostile feelings.

This process of transference and countertransference underscores the need to discuss and work through your feelings with a colleague or supervisor. This work is difficult and emotionally provoking. Thus, you need to ensure clear boundaries in order to provide the appropriate treatment needed.

Pearlman and Saakvitne pointed out in their book *Trauma and the Therapist* (1995) that few training programs for mental health professionals offer education about psychological trauma and the complex process of trauma therapy, such as education on understanding and using transference and countertransference. They cautioned that the lack of information and training increases the likelihood that therapists will impose their needs and conflicts on their clients and psychotherapies.

Pearlman and Saakvitne (1995) covered a broad range of issues for the therapist working with survivors of childhood sexual abuse. They addressed specific countertransference issues that arise in intensive psychotherapy with incest survivors as well as the issue of therapist self-care—including supervision and consultation for trauma therapies and ameliorating vicarious traumatization. They strongly suggested supervision or consultation when doing trauma work—a recommendation for all therapists doing psychotherapeutic work in general.

In addition to the transference issues just discussed, the adolescent is going through normal hormonal changes and identity issues. It is easy for teens to misinterpret caring intentions of the therapist. In addition, therapists who are not clear on their own boundaries may find themselves attracted to the teen they are treating. Therefore, it is critical that you maintain appropriate boundaries and ethical standards at all times.

This book has been designed to delve much deeper into an explanation of each phase of the healing process as each chapter is introduced. The introductions are followed by detailed instructions for how to organize each activity and by an explanation for each activity.

Case studies have been included in each chapter to clarify how some of the activities have been used in actual therapy situations. We have given a brief case history, an example of the dialogue between the therapist and the teenager during the activity, and clinical impressions. We have also included some drawings that relate to actual therapy sessions. Names, characteristics, and circumstances have been altered to protect the adolescents' identities.

As stated previously, the chapters have been organized to proceed through the healing process. However, each individual enters therapy at a different stage in his or her recovery. Therefore, certain chapters or activities may not seem needed or specific to a particular adolescent's issues. It is up to you and the treatment goals set forth by you and the group or individual to dictate which activities will be needed. As stated previously, these activities should be viewed as an adjunct to other forms of therapeutic intervention.

It is important to remember that no one should ever be forced to engage in an activity. Pressure may serve to retraumatize the already traumatized adolescent. Unwillingness may alert you to the need to concentrate on the less abuse-focused activities found in Chapters 2 through 4. We hope this will assist you in your therapy with abused adolescents.

Acknowledgments

We would like to take this opportunity to thank all of our colleagues and friends who assisted or supported us in the creation of this book. The idea of this book orginated from the completion of our last book, Treatment Strategies for Abused Children: From Victim to Survivor. Traci and I realized that we needed to extend our work to include adolescents. We welcomed Sage Bergstrom with open arms in this endeavor. She added a new perspective and fresh mind to the process.

First of all we want to thank Bill Friedrich for agreeing to write the Forward to our book. He has been a continual source of professional excellence. We are of like minds when it comes to our commitment to abused children. We also want to thank many others who have inspired our work in this field: John Briere, Elaina Gil, Diana Elliott, Lucy Berliner, Kee MacFarlane, David Corwin, David Finkelhor, Roland Summit, and Judith Becker. We thank them for continuing to enrich our field. They represent just a few from a long list of wonderful professionals we have met through the American Professional Society on the Abuse of Children (APSAC). We also benefitted from the work of Lenore Terr and Christine Courtois on the effects of trauma.

Jon Conte was formidable in the organization of our last book, which served as a model for this book. We thank him for his continued support and for his guidance as our professional editor for the Interpersonal Violence Series.

Again, thanks to C. Terry Hendrix for believing in this book from its conception.

A special thanks is extended to Len Karp for his support, humor and snacks, as we all congregated on Sundays to work at Cheryl's and Len's house. We would also like to thank our families for continuing to be a source of moral support.

Cheryl L. Karp
Traci L. Butler
Sage C. Bergstrom

1

Adolescent Social and Sexual Development

To understand and appreciate the devastating effects that abuse has on adolescents, it is best to review normal adolescent social and sexual development as well as certain issues specific to the emergence of adolescence. As children progress from infancy to adulthood, they move through dynamic and ever-changing periods. What happens during this process has a critical effect on future functioning. Those persons who interact with the child during these critical years will surely have a significant impact on later development through the life span (Helfer, 1987).

❑ Overview of Normal Sexual Development

There has been a concerted effort in the last decade to educate therapists and parents about the "red flags" associated with child sexual abuse. But we have often neglected to educate others about

1

what constitutes normal sexual development. In our earlier book *Treatment Strategies for Abused Children* (Karp & Butler, 1996), we provided an overview of normal sexual development to address this concern. In our work with abused adolescents, we have encountered a similar problem. We asked ourselves what developmental issues would be important to address when working with abused teens.

In addition to outlining normal adolescent sexual development, we will address other issues pertinent to adolescent development. Adolescence is the stage at which social interactions are central. In addition, gay and lesbian issues emerge. Because the issues of male and female adolescents sometimes differ along gender lines, gender differences surrounding abuse issues are also of concern. Knowing the specifics of abnormal and abusive sexual behavior is imperative in working with abused adolescents. We have also included a section on parental guidance in this chapter.

As stated in our previous book, sexual development, like psychosocial and cognitive development, occurs in progressive stages (Karp & Butler, 1996). With regard to sexual capacity, from birth children have occasional erections or vaginal secretions, and by the age of 5 any child is capable of autoerotic experiences (Martinson, 1991). In addition, cultural norms come into play when evaluating what is normal versus abnormal sexual development. According to Martinson (1991),

> Each child's development will be markedly influenced by the cultural norms and expectations, familial interactions and values, and the interpersonal experiences encountered. . . . Organic capacities, cognitive development and integration, and intrapsychic influences further determine the rate and extent of development of the sexual capacity. (p. 58)

Latency-aged children (7-12 years) engage in a range of sexual interests. They continue to have peer contact in school, they may also begin to experiment with sexual behaviors, and they may have alternating periods of disinhibition and inhibition (Gil & Johnson, 1993, pp. 21-40). Children in this age group vary a great deal. The term *latency* is rather misleading in that this is not a stage when girls or boys are truly "dormant." According to Everstine and Everstine (1989),

Especially from the age of nine or ten, most boys engage in a rich form of experimentation that is best characterized as 'silent sex.' Excited by fantasy but lost in perplexity, the boy muses for long hours on the subject, inventing vague theories of the differences between males and females. (p. 129)

According to Morris (1997), researchers suggest that children of this general age group may appear less interested in sexual topics because they have learned adult rules about repressing sexual matters and have therefore become more secretive and private about their sexual thoughts, feelings, and behavior. During this time, most children enter puberty.

Developmentally, preadolescents (10-12 years) are focused on establishing relationships with peers. Many preadolescents, and certainly adolescents (13-18 years), engage in sexual activity with peers, including open-mouth kissing, sexual fondling, simulated intercourse, sexual penetration behaviors, and intercourse (Cunningham & MacFarlane, 1991; Gil, 1991). Adolescents and some preadolescents find themselves *falling in love.*

According to Friedrich (1990), children are likely to assume cultural norms and restraints because they are subject to nonfamilial socialization experiences, even if their families possess liberal sexual/nudity values. Due to all the moral, religious, and health restrictions on sexuality, many children avoid penile/genital contact and engage in cunnilingus and fellatio, while other children fear and/or avoid all sexual contact until much later (Gil & Johnson, 1993, pp. 21-40).

Rutter (1971) reported a gradual increase in masturbation from the prepubescent years to the advent of adolescence, ranging from about 10% at age 7 to about 80% at 13 years of age. He also noted an increase in sexual play from about 5% at 5 years of age to about 65% at 13 years of age. According to Friedrich (1990), during adolescence there is also a marked increase in sexual activity and interest for both sexes. Morris (1997) pointed out that despite strong sociocultural prohibitions, masturbation soon becomes the primary sexual activity for most adolescents.

Adolescence is often described as a time of transition into adulthood. This can be a trying time for the teenager because he or she is no longer viewed as a "child" but is not truly regarded as an "adult."

This can cause internal conflict as the adolescent strives to separate and individuate from the parent figure. In addition, the advent of adolescence signals the onset of puberty, which denotes changes in sexual development.

The changes in sexual development brought on by puberty result in physical metamorphoses that can be a source of concern, anxiety, and preoccupation for many teens. The timing, rate of pubertal changes, and type of physical change experienced may have differential effects, especially on the female adolescent's self-image and self-esteem (Bukowski, Sippola, & Brender, 1993). Society's obsession with the "perfect" body has resulted in the quest for "thinness" as reflecting "beauty." For the male adolescent, the impact of changes in physical maturation on the self-concept appears to be generally positive, most likely due to society's attitude toward masculine characteristics (Bukowski et al., 1993).

Sexual development in adolescence is frequently conceptualized very narrowly, denoting physical changes or behavioral/interpersonal changes that are related to puberty (Bukowski et al., 1993). Accordingly, sexuality begins at puberty and is largely a physical or behavioral construct. However, Bukowski et al. (1993) contended that sexuality and sexual development are processes that begin at birth and continue across the life span and are embedded within the broader context of interpersonal relations. They saw sexual development as being largely a "synthetic" process, meaning that it derives from the individual's synthesis, or integration, of many dimensions of experience, including feelings of sexual desire and interpersonal attraction, sense of morality, social convention, interpersonal security, and view of others as sexual beings who have their own needs, desires, and rights. Bukowski et al. (1993) proposed that a healthy sense of sexuality includes:

1. Learning about intimacy through interaction with peers;
2. Developing an understanding of personal roles and relationships, both within and outside of the family;
3. Revising or adapting one's body schema to changes in physical size, shape, and capabilities, especially during early adolescence;
4. Adjusting to erotic feelings and experiences and integrating them into one's life;

5. Learning about societal standards and practices regarding sexual expression;
6. Developing an understanding and appreciation of reproductive processes. (p. 86)

Puberty is generally marked by the occurrence of reproductive maturation. The male testes begin to produce sperm, and the female begins to ovulate. Menarche is the single readily identifiable event that denotes the onset of puberty for females. This normally occurs between the ages of 10 and 16 years. *Secondary sex characteristics* also begin to appear during puberty, such as breasts and pubic hair for females (Morris, 1997).

The onset of puberty for the male is more subtle and is mostly marked by emerging *secondary sex characteristics* (Morris, 1997). The most prominent changes include the development of facial, pubic, and other body hair, as well as a lowering of the voice due to the lengthening of the vocal cords. According to Morris (1997),

> During puberty, the hypothalamus and the pituitary glands combine to stimulate the maturing testes into producing sperm capable of reproduction. The testes are also stimulated to produce large amounts of testosterone, which is primarily responsible for the secondary sex characteristics as well as the enlargement of the testes and the shaft of the penis. (p. 19)

This is also when most males experience a growth spurt, including an increase in height, weight, musculature, and physical strength.

Other signs of sexual maturity for the male during adolescence may include "wet dreams" (nocturnal emissions), the beginning of masturbation to ejaculation, and an increased interest in the opposite sex. Morris (1997) cited the common descriptions of adolescent males during puberty as "raging hormone machines" or "hormones on wheels" to emphasize the sudden increase in hormones at puberty.

Although Morris (1997) pointed out that hormones play a key role in the final development of one's gender, he questioned whether sex hormones also regulate human sexual feelings and behavior. He noted that the answer to this question is not clear because most research in this area is with lower animals and may not generalize to humans. Research does indicate that for adolescent males, free (circulating) testosterone levels seem to predict sexual interest, masturbation rates, and the early onset of sexual intercourse (Udry, 1988; Udry & Billy, 1987; Udry, Billy, Morris, Groff, & Raj, 1985).

The above citations only serve to illustrate the importance of having a general knowledge of adolescent sexual development in order to better understand the significance of hormones when approaching male and female abused adolescents during therapy. A general understanding of the role that hormone development plays during adolescence will enhance the understanding of adolescent behavior, which in turn, furthers therapy. The importance of hormone development and its effect on aggression and aggressive sexual behavior have also been studied. This is not the context in which to explore these findings, but for more information the reader is referred to Morris's (1997) book, *The Male Heterosexual*, as well as Barbaree, Marshall, and Hudson's (1993) text *The Juvenile Sex Offender*.

❑ Gay and Lesbian Issues

Though most of the above experiences are heterosexual, it is common for preadolescents and adolescents to have some same-gender sexual experiences (Friedrich, 1990; Kinsey, Pomeroy, Martin, & Gebhard, 1953; Morris, 1997). During this stage of development, many teens begin to suspect that they are gay, lesbian, or bisexual. Kinsey's landmark works, *Sexual Behavior in the Human Male* (Kinsey, Pomeroy, & Martin, 1948) and *Sexual Behavior in the Human Female* (Kinsey et al., 1953), promoted the view that human sexuality lies on a continuum. Kinsey posited, on the basis of his research, that very few adults were exclusively hetero- or homosexual in their behavior, no matter how they chose to label themselves; most people fell somewhere in between.

As therapists working with abused adolescents, we believe it is crucial to present a nonjudgmental stance toward issues of sexual orientation. It is important to keep in mind that sexual orientation is an integral part of personality.

In 1968, the American Psychiatric Association removed homosexuality from its diagnostic manual of mental disorders, saying that homosexuality per se did not in and of itself imply any impairment in judgment, stability, reliability, or general social or vocational capabilities (American Psychiatric Association, 1968). However, stereotypes, ignorance, and misinformation still create an environment in which discrimination can thrive. Fear of rejection by peers and parents has placed many adolescents at risk not only for low self-esteem but also for suicidal ideation and behaviors. Therapists are in a particularly good position to replace error with knowledge and to challenge damaging myths that will certainly interfere with their treatment of abused adolescents. Many clinicians who regarded homosexuality as a mental illness encouraged their adolescent and adult clients to become heterosexual as a way to relieve the client's guilt and anxiety. The possibility that homophobia could be the cause of this anguish was not acknowledged (Bergstrom & Cruz, 1980).

According to Roche (1983), lesbian and gay male adolescents are all too aware of the reception awaiting them on "coming out." They know that many child care workers and clinicians believe that homosexuality is an illness or, at best, an arrested developmental stage. When adolescents fear rejection, they are on guard, and such wariness complicates their treatment. Frequently, teens report that the mere presence of literature that addresses their lifestyle has been sufficient to notify them that they have finally found a sensitive and accepting source of help.

Teenage girls and boys may be loath to disclose any sexual abuse by someone of the same sex if they fear that peers and adults will think they have become gay as a result. Their own internalized homophobia may also cause intense shame and guilt. A corollary to this is the myth that many women become lesbian because they have been abused by men.

The etiology of sexual orientation is not nearly as important as the viability of the adolescent's daily life. The focus of any discussion of identity development should be on how to relate to oneself and others in a responsible manner. The focus in survivor group treatment should be on the common human experience of having been abused rather than on the issue of sexual orientation. For these reasons, gay and heterosexual adolescents can be treated in the same abuse-focused group (Crowder, 1995).

At the present time, no one clearly knows why heterosexuals are heterosexual and homosexuals homosexual, although many theories abound (Barbaree et al., 1993; Bergstrom & Cruz, 1980; Morris, 1997). Morris (1997) pointed out that a growing body of research suggests a strong genetic biologic connection to homosexuality. Twin and other family member studies suggest a possible genetic link within the family.

Roche (1983) commented that in planning treatment, self-professed lesbian and gay male adolescents need to be distinguished from those who have been referred because they have been engaged in same-sex behavior such as prostituting or "hustling." Homosexual behaviors may be considered symptomatic of an underlying gay orientation or confused sexual identity. But the secondary gains of these behaviors may exist regardless of the adolescent's sexual orientation. These gains may be a sense of being valued and needed (especially if the adolescent has been sexually abused when younger) or may be monetary. Alcohol and other drug (AOD) abuse is one way to cope with personal conflict due to abuse, and the therapist should realize that many substance abusers have found prostitution a profitable way to pay for their habit, regardless of their sexual orientation.

When teens who have been acting out sexually come for therapy, it is very important for the therapist to make it clear that the relationship will be nonsexual. If the teen is in a residential treatment center (RTC), he or she should also be aware that any adult working for the facility will maintain a supportive but nonsexual relationship with him or her. Adolescents need to be provided with information on the facility's grievance procedure as well as how to contact the local Child Protective Services office. In and of itself, this message can be therapeutic because boundaries are being spelled out so that the adolescent does not have to worry about interpreting the motives of the facility staff (Roche, 1983). However, on being told this, some sexualized teens may withdraw because their self-worth has been so closely tied with providing others with sexual gratification. Others may realize they will not be able to manipulate their therapist and may prefer to leave treatment, knowing they will not have control over the relationship. They may experience nonsexual closeness with their therapist and/or peers as risky.

❑ Issues to Consider in Treating Male Versus Female Victims

Many researchers in the field of child maltreatment have given special thought to male survivors of sexual abuse (Bolton, Morris, & MacEachron, 1989; Crowder, 1995; Friedrich, 1991, 1995; Everstine & Everstine, 1989; Hunter, 1989; Morris, 1997). In her book *Opening the Door* (1995), Adrienne Crowder discussed her findings based on clinical contributions from 41 therapists who had worked with male survivors of sexual abuse, both adolescent and adult. Based on these findings, she developed a treatment model for adolescent and adult male survivors, with some emphasis on male adolescents in particular.

According to Crowder (1995), current research substantiates that certain significant differences exist between the sexual victimization of males and that of females. These concern the nature of the experience itself as well as how the experience is understood and integrated. Awareness of these factors is important in designing and implementing treatment strategies. Cultural beliefs and stereotypes of femininity and masculinity may have the following impacts on the male adolescent sexual abuse victim:

- He may see himself as less than male (emasculation).
- He may see himself as a "woman" (feminized) as being powerless (flawed).
- He may see himself as being sexually interested in males (homosexual).

None of these interpretations of victimization is useful for male teens when working on trauma (Crowder, 1995).

Another belief the adolescent male may have internalized is that no matter what, all sexual activity is good for males. When a sexually mature female victimizes a younger, less mature male, this may be seen as "scoring" by his peers. Films portraying sexual abuse of males by females in a romantic light or as an initiation into the grown-up world of sexuality are a powerful reinforcement of this belief for a young man. Teens may not want to accept that the female abuser's behavior gratified her needs rather than their own. Even if the teen does not consciously view his experience negatively, it still affects him negatively, influencing his subsequent behavior and relationships. A teenage girl is much more likely to see her victimization as harmful and as an affront to her personhood. Another misleading belief is the stereotype of female "innocence." Nurturing qualities of women in general and mothers in particular make the idea of their touch being sexualized unthinkable to many, especially children (Crowder, 1995).

The belief that male victims automatically become perpetrators may certainly prevent some male victims from disclosing their abuse. This adds to the guilt to the guilt and shame that not only were they abused but they could become just like the person who abused them, an thinkable proposition. For male victims who have also perpetrated abuse, the scenario may change. Because societal norms relating to control and power issues reinforce the difficulty for male victims of describing themselves as having been in a vulnerable position, it may actually be safer for them to discuss any perpetrating behaviors they may have engaged in rather than their victimization.

Males are much less likely to talk about their abuse experiences because "being a victim is a countercultural experience for a man" (Crowder, 1995, p. 37). Thus, men tend not to seek out support from peers or counseling or therapy. Adolescent boys in treatment probably have not made any connection between their negative, acting-out behaviors and their abuse. More than likely, these negative behaviors brought them to treatment in the first place.

According to Friedrich (1990, 1995), group therapy with peers is highly recommended because of the need to break down isolation for both male and female victims. Males should be encouraged to relate to each other outside of group as well. In therapy, the focus for boys may have to do with learning how to deal with anger constructively before moving into emotions such as shame, guilt, and grief. For teenage girls, who often present as depressed and self-harming, the focus may be on drawing out their rage. For both teenage boys and girls, developing assertiveness skills will help them in managing their anger.

Both females and males are victimized more often by adult males than by adult females (Finkelhor, 1986; Morris, 1997). This means that males are victimized by their own sex more than females are, although Morris (1997) pointed out that female abuse of males is more common than once thought. Homophobic attitudes in society may make it more difficult for a male teen molested by an adult male to disclose. (During the intake stage for assessing potential group members, attention needs to be paid to overtly homophobic attitudes. A homophobic group member would make it difficult for peers to disclose in group.)

Other factors that may influence the treatment of male victims, according to Crowder (1995), include the finding that boys are more likely than girls to be victimized by someone outside the family. In one study, 83% of abusers were nonfamily members (Finkelhor, 1984). These incidents are usually not accepted by Child Protective Services (CPS), but rather reported to police. Adult authority figures outside the home, such as babysitters, coaches, teachers, scout leaders, and family "friends," more often abuse males than do family members. Another finding of Crowder's was that boys who live in single-mother households are more frequently abused than girls who live in these households.

Interestingly, Crowder (1995) noted in research cited by Finkelhor (1984) that when a girl reports sexual abuse occurring within the family, 65% of the time she will be the only reported victim, whereas if a boy is abused within the family, 60% of the time there will be another victim. Finkelhor also learned that boys were more likely to be physically abused along with the sexual abuse. Girls are more likely to be taken out of the home and placed in protective custody than are boys (Finkelhor, 1984; Pierce & Pierce, 1985; Vander May, 1988). Females receive counseling more frequently and receive it for a longer period of time than males (Vander May, 1988).

Crowder (1995) mentioned that there is little information on the impact of abuse or models of treatment for males. Before Crowder's book appeared, Friedrich (1990) had also commented that as of that date, no studies existed that could document the success of individual therapy with sexually abused children (p. 132). However, since Crowder and Friedrich expressed this concern, Friedrich's newest book, *Psychotherapy With Sexually Abused Boys: An Integrated Approach* (1995), has offered an integrated model of therapy to address treatment needs for sexually abused boys and adolescents. This excellent treatise offers individual, group, and family therapy techniques for sexually abused males. Although Friedrich noted that his model is still not tested or empirically validated, it reveals much promise and is based on rich clinical theory and empirically validated approaches.

For aggressively acting-out male teens, we have found that identifying fantasies of anger through drawing and writing can be a powerful adjunct to talking therapy. These nonverbal modalities may be less threatening for the male victim, relieving him of the pressure he feels to self-disclose directly in front of his therapist or peers. In the Foreword to Karp & Butler's (1996) book, Friedrich stated that "successful therapy with children and adolescents who have difficulty talking about trauma oftentimes needs to be nonverbal and activity-based" (p. ix).

Activities in Chapter 3 of this book (e.g., "Feelings Charade") can aid male teen victims in discovering a range of emotions. Developing assertiveness skills will also help them in managing their anger. Reading stories and watching videos that deal with childhood abuse, violence in dating relationships, communication skills, and issues related to cultural norms and stereotypes may also serve as nonthreatening strategies to encourage self-disclosure.

❏ Abnormal and Abusive Sexual Behavior

Abnormal sexual behavior for young school-age children (5-7 years) would be sexual penetration, genital kissing or oral copulation, and simulated intercourse (Cunningham & MacFarlane, 1991), and abnormal sexual behavior for preadolescents and adolescents would include sexual play with younger children, as well as coercive, exploitive, or aggressive sex with same-age peers (Sgroi, 1988). Friedrich (1990) reported that data from a normative sample of approximately 900 children aged 2 to 12 years indicated that specifically sexual behaviors, such as attempting intercourse, inserting objects in the vagina or rectum, and touching breasts of adults were unusual in normal, nonabused children.

Regardless of a child's age, abusive sexual behavior is considered abnormal. In their preliminary report (National Adolescent Perpetrator Network, 1988), the Task Force on Juvenile Sexual Offending stated:

> Sexual interactions involving children with peers or younger children are problematic if the relationship is *coercive, exploitive* or *aggressive* or *threatens the physical or psychological well-being of either participant.* . . . The exploitive nature of child sexual offending is measured in terms of size and age differential; power or authority differential; lack of equality and consent; and threats, violence or aggression. (p. 42)

Sgroi (1988) used similar criteria in suggesting that answers to the following questions indicate whether a sexual activity may be considered abusive:

- What are the power positions of the participants?
- Is force or intimidation used?
- Is ritual or sadistic abuse involved?
- Was secrecy involved?
- How developmentally appropriate are the sexual acts?

Johnson (Gil and Johnson, 1993) devised a *continuum* of sexual disturbance for children 12 and under who have intact reality testing and are not considered developmentally delayed. Johnson divided these children into four groups. Group I included children who engage in normal childhood sexual exploration, Group II included sexually reactive children, Group III included children with extensive mutual sexual behaviors, and Group 4 included children who molest other children.

If you spend very much time working with sexually abused children or adolescents abused as young children, you may want to read more about these four groups. It has been our experience that sexually abused children often gravitate to each other and may engage in behaviors consistent with the last three groups mentioned above. To effectively treat and provide comprehensive therapeutic care for these children, a clear understanding of each group and the behaviors consistent with each group is necessary.

An informative compilation of chapters written by experts in the field of adolescent sex offenders is Barbaree et al.'s *The Juvenile Sex Offender* (1993). This text covers a broad range of topics from normative sexual development to sexual assault through the life span, attachment bonds, cognitive-behavioral treatment of the juvenile sex offender, the relationship between substance use and abuse and sexual offending, pharmacological treatment of the adolescent sex offender, and relapse prevention. If you plan on working with reactive abusers or if you also work with adolescent perpetrators, the above book is strongly suggested.

❏ **Parental Guidance**

As children enter adolescence, their history of sexual development follows them. Probably one of the most critical factors in child sexual development is the level of parental guidance. Parents play an important role in providing values about sexuality to their children. According to Gil and Johnson (1993), when parents view sex as dirty, inappropriate, or secretive, they may set rigid and restrictive limits on healthy curiosity, self-exploration, and questions. When children are punished, chastised, or humiliated for appropriate sexual exploration, they may begin to associate sex with shame or guilt.

Some parents may be oversexualized, creating a sexualized environment. Though it may not always be sexualized behavior, adult nudity or lack of appropriate boundaries can have a detrimental effect on a child's sexuality. Other parents may be undersexualized, creating an environment in which sex is taboo. Households where children never see parents behaving affectionately render a child naive about appropriate displays of affection. Either polarity can negatively affect the child's healthy sexual development.

Children and adolescents need an open environment in which they can ask questions and learn about sexuality. We all know that if children cannot find the answers at home, they will turn to their peer group or their own experimentation for answers. By the time they reach adolescence, the knowledge and mores provided by the parents and peer group are well entrenched. However, there are still many issues to be raised by parents. Teens may have questions regarding sexuality and sexual orientation. Although there are classes in most schools that address sexuality and sex education issues such as sexually transmitted diseases (STDs) and AIDS awareness, parents should be available to discuss these important issues personally with their children.

Parents of gay and lesbian teens who desire additional information about gay and lesbian issues may find Parents and Friends of Lesbian and Gays (PFLAG) to be a helpful resource (1-202-638-4200).

PHASE I

Establishing Therapeutic Rapport

2

Who Am I?
Image Building, Goal Setting,
and Therapeutic Trust

Developing rapport and building a therapeutic alliance with the abused/traumatized adolescent is an important goal early in the therapeutic relationship (Haugaard & Reppucci, 1988, pp. 237-238). Since most adolescent victims do not voluntarily seek out a therapist, rapport building can be a difficult task. In addition, adolescents are struggling with separation and individuation issues, and this tends to alienate them from adult relationships. They may also feel that they are not included in decision making; thus, they may seek autonomy from the adult world. These factors make the task of developing a therapeutic relationship difficult.

Abused adolescents may initially view the therapist as another adult attempting to dominate or control them. For those adolescents who were abused in early childhood, the therapeutic relationship may trigger a sense of being dominated, which in the past led to their victimization. Therefore, it is important to give plenty of time for a positive therapeutic relationship to develop. It is also important to understand that teens with an early childhood abusive history often suffer ongoing impaired ability to trust.

Children who have been abused sexually, physically, or emotionally experience severe damage to their self-esteem. Their sense of self is fragmented, and they are often filled with self-hate, guilt, and confusion. They defend against these horrible emotions by suppressing them—pushing the feelings down deep inside—or by acting them out. By the time these children reach adolescence, such defenses may be firmly ingrained.

The abused individual will often rely on unhealthy coping mechanisms such as *dissociation, minimization, denial, or anger* to defend against the overwhelming emotions that are difficult to understand. Dissociation allows the individual to separate or split off from his or her emotions, providing a sense of protection from difficult experiences. The fourth edition of the *Diagnostic and Statistical Manual of Mental Disorders* (*DSM-IV*; American Psychiatric Association, 1994) defined *dissociation* as "a disruption in the usual integrated functions of consciousness, memory, identity, or perception of the environment. The disturbance may be sudden or gradual, transient or chronic" (p. 477).

It is important to have a basic understanding of dissociation because many traumatized adolescents do exhibit symptoms associated with this disorder that may interfere with the rapport-building phase of therapy. According to Gil (1993), abused children often report feelings of depersonalization and psychogenic amnesia for prior events. You may see this behavior as just "staring off into space" or "spacing out." Those who dissociate will be unable to hear, process, or understand what is being discussed in either group or individual therapy. Therefore, if an adolescent is often not attentive, you may need to assess for a dissociative disorder.

Developing a common language to cue victims about their dissociative states can be helpful, such as reminding them to stay in the here and now. It is important to point out that this was a survival skill that worked very well at one point in time but that it is not so helpful now. The goal is to help each individual gain a sense of mastery over this coping skill.

You may find as your therapeutic rapport becomes stronger with the adolescent that he or she may be more willing to share what is being experienced internally. This willingness may allow you, as the therapist, to find more effective ways to provide cues and will encourage the teen to be part of that process.

As stated above, the abused victim may use denial or anger to cope with the traumatic experiences. A victim who is in a state of denial may refuse to admit that anything has actually occurred. This person needs to see everything as "normal." This state of denial not only helps the individual to protect the people he or she loves but allows him or her to keep the experiences at a distance, providing a false sense of control.

Acting-out adolescents who are dissociative or in denial may be suffering from Post-Traumatic Stress Disorder. They may be acting out the violent experiences or the confusion and turmoil that they are feeling internally. These teenagers are frequently labeled as having Oppositional Defiant Disorder, Conduct Disorder, or Attention-Deficit/Hyperactivity Disorder (see American Psychiatric Association, 1994, for a proper definition of these disorders). While their behaviors may be consistent with these disorders, it is also possible that the effects of the trauma has resulted in this display or behavior. The abused adolescent may also turn to alcohol or other drugs (AODs) as a strategy to cope with the internal chaos. Therefore, it is important to use caution when labeling or diagnosing abused adolescents on the basis of their seemingly self-destructive actions.

Traumatized individuals frequently feel out of control and powerless. They are not clear on just who they are. There is typically a lack of trust in oneself and others, especially among adolescents who experienced trauma in the first 5 years of life, causing disrupted ability to form attachments. This disrupted ability to form attachments results in confusion regarding the essence of trust. The peer group is such a strong force at this time in development that abused adolescents frequently find themselves in problematic relationships. They may give up too much power to their peer group (e.g., a gang); place all their trust in one "love" interest, which may result in an abusive relationship; become pregnant; or acquire a sexually transmitted disease (STD). They may also tend to isolate themselves to guard against being hurt.

Traumatized teens also may turn to various maladaptive means of coping with their own internal chaos. Overeating, anorexia nervosa,

AOD use, self-mutilation, or sexual acting out are just some of the behaviors used to numb feelings of rage, shame, or despair and may be a teen's only form of nurturance. Therefore, the way the teens see themselves is a good barometer of where they are in recovery.

Typically, the traumatized adolescent is struggling with so many issues that developing the therapeutic relationship is a difficult and time-consuming process. Therefore, building a solid foundation of trust is paramount. This chapter is designed to begin building rapport in nonthreatening ways. The exercises will focus on helping the adolescent explore his or her own image as well as how he or she sees him- or herself in relation to others.

The abused individual often has a fragmented sense of self. Our hope is that the adolescent will build a rapport with you as the therapist so that movement through the more painful aspects of trauma recovery will be achievable. The process becomes one of starting from the ground floor and repairing the sense of self.

The following activities are designed to assist adolescents in exploring who they are in relation to their family and to begin working on individual goal setting. As the therapist working with the teen, you are free to select the activities that seem to best facilitate growth. However, we have organized the activities in a way we think follows a logical progression to address therapeutic needs.

A few case studies have been included to clarify how some of these activities have been used in actual therapy situations. We have given a brief case history, an example of dialogue between the therapist and adolescent during the activity, and clinical impressions.

If you find that the teen you are working with is extremely resistant, you may want to supplement the activities listed with some of your own in an effort to meet individual therapeutic needs. We realize that additional time may be necessary on any given therapeutic goal in the treatment process.

As you work through the activities in this chapter, you are building the therapeutic foundation necessary to process through more difficult stages of healing, which will be addressed in later chapters. It is unlikely that the abused adolescent will experience a high level of stress when involved with the activities in this chapter. However, if he or she does exhibit evidence of distress, proceed slowly and cautiously through the activities.

It is important to engage in thorough processing of thoughts and feelings as you move forward in the healing process. At the end of several of the activity descriptions in this manual, you will find a section called "Processing." Our suggestions in the processing section are general. You will most likely add your own ideas as you get to know the adolescent.

The *Activity Book* that accompanies this manual includes a section entitled, "Teen Talk" for each chapter. The purpose of this section is to introduce each chapter in adolescent-appropriate language. The *Activity Book* is filled with various activities that will assist the teen in working through traumatic experiences. It also provides the adolescent survivor with tangible evidence of the work that he or she accomplished during the healing process.

❏ **Activity #1: My Biography**

Objective: To build therapeutic rapport with the adolescent and, if used in a group, among peers.

The activity is designed to get your relationship started and to enable you to learn something about how the adolescent views his or her history. We have included factual questions for you to ask, but mostly it is designed to reflect the adolescent's perceptions of his or her history. This activity accomplishes two goals in building a therapeutic relationship. First, it provides additional information about the adolescent. Second, it is a nonthreatening means to begin the process of rapport building and communication.

In individual therapy (as well as in group), a teen may be very resistant to engage in any activity that is verbally oriented or involves directly sharing material about oneself, however nonthreatening the therapist may perceive the material to be. Teens may be articulate but carefully avoid any mention of why they are in therapy. They may make statements such as "I don't even know why I'm here," "That's in the past, I've forgotten all about it," or "Why do you need to know this stupid stuff, anyway?" They may share little, if any, information about their lives. Many teens, having carried the burden of their abuse for so many years, have dissociated from their anger, shame, and grief. They may express much anger but deny that this is worth working on. They will push you away in a variety of ways. How do we establish trust and a therapeutic bond with these highly defended individuals? It can be a challenging job.

If you have additional questions that you want to include, feel free to add them to the instructions to the adolescent. The more you can engage in a direct dialogue over nonthreatening material, the better the therapeutic bond becomes. This makes it much easier when you get to more difficult material later in the therapeutic process.

Ages: Adolescents between the ages of 13 and 18 years should be able to respond to all of the questions in this activity. Most teens will be able to complete the autobiography on their own. Severely learning-disabled adolescents who have difficulties reading or writing may need you to read the instructions and have you record their history or, if in a group, may ask their peers for help.

Materials Needed: Activity sheet and pencil.

Instructions: Instruct the teen to read the instructions in the *Activity Book* and to write their biography in the space provided. As stated previously, if the adolescent is severely learning disabled and is unable to complete this on his or her own, you may have him or her dictate the history to you or work with a peer.

A common question from teens may be, "Should I put down my trauma issues?" Reassure them that there will be ample opportunity later to discuss those issues; however, they may choose to discuss the issues at this point if they wish, and they can be as nonspecific as they like.

If adolescents are pushed too early to reveal their abuse histories, they may feel that their boundaries have been violated. Teens who ask if they "should" include the trauma history may be trying to please you, for they usually know, after all, why they are in therapy. The idea here is to let survivors know that it is okay to have boundaries for sharing personal information and that part of the recovery process is to practice having boundaries in order to learn what these are for each person. Survivors must come to understand the concept and practice of trusting oneself before they are truly able to trust others. When the therapist models respecting the teen's boundaries, the development of trust and therapeutic rapport is aided tremendously. In a group situation, the therapist can also model and teach how peers can respect each other's boundaries. (An activity for learning about physical space/boundaries will be included in Chapter 4.)

Once the biography is completed, you will need to go over it together. This provides a good opportunity to engage in positive dialogue.

Note: Before beginning this activity, an assessment of the teen's reading and writing skills is important. It would be countertherapeutic to give the adolescent a task that was beyond his or her functioning level because he or she would become too frustrated with the activity and your requests. You can assess the teen's functioning level informally, or you can ask the parent (or guardian) if there is a history of learning difficulties or disabilities.

Processing: Once the adolescent is finished, the therapist and teen should review the biography. While reviewing the biography, you may want to ask additional questions, especially if the biography is terse. The important thing to remember in completing this activity is that the goal is to establish rapport. The more you can engage with the adolescent, the stronger the therapeutic bond.

In reviewing the biography, you should note which questions the teen is hesitant to answer or may not even know how to answer. Some teens make rather superficial replies, whereas others may "spill their guts." The latter group will be noted to have permeable boundaries and perhaps either to have blocked affect or to be easily overwhelmed by their emotional associations to the material. You may ask such teens to rewrite their biography, leaving out the volatile material for now.

Note: For teens who are resistant to completing their biography, other, less threatening "icebreakers," such as "Say one word about your past, present, and future," may be more effective. For others, an alternative technique using "play" may be less threatening. The case example cited below illustrates this scenario.

Case Example: *Jeanine*

Brief Case History: Jeanine was a 13-year-old Asian American teen sent to an adolescent treatment facility from out of state. She lived with her mother and was an only child. Her parents were in the process of getting divorced for the second time. Jeanine had been seeing a number of psychiatrists and psychologists in outpatient treatment on and off for a number of years, but treatment had been unsuccessful. The mother claimed that because Jeanine "did not remember" her early sexual abuse by her paternal uncle, it had had no effect on her. Jeanine did remember being beaten by this uncle and thrown across the room. Jeanine's mother defensively explained this history as "discipline." Jeanine had begun hitting her mother, and recently this had escalated to the point that her mother felt she could no longer control her. Jeanine had no friends at home, having alienated schoolmates by either hitting them or isolating herself.

On interview, Jeanine was an attractive young adolescent who looked to be about 11 years old. Her IQ was above average, and she apparently had no learning disabilities. She answered questions tersely, showed no spontaneity, and appeared quite depressed. She did admit she "didn't like" her uncle but declined to elaborate. Jeanine let it be known that she was "mad" at the therapist for even asking her any questions about her life.

Jeanine was given Activity #1, "My Biography," to complete, but she refused to answer the questions. It was decided that a less threatening activity would be used to gain therapeutic rapport before this activity was initiated again.

Example of Alternative to Activity #1: Rapport Building Through Play: As stated above, Jeanine refused to complete her biography. Therefore, she was asked to come to a therapy session to "play." Because Jeanine had previously said she had no friends and because she appeared very passive and despondent, it was hard to know if Jeanine would even be willing to "play." However, the therapist was in for a surprise. On entering the office, Jeanine looked around for a second, then ran to the doll house. She rapidly took each piece of furniture and each doll out, then very carefully and methodically rearranged each room. The dolls were placed on their beds, with their clothes on. A baby in a cradle was placed in the parent's bedroom. As the therapist silently watched, Jeanine began to talk:

Jeanine It's okay, you can talk.
Therapist What would you like me to talk about?
J   Let's play a game!

   (Jeanine ran to the cabinet, picked out the "ungame," and brought it to the table.)

J   Let's see how to play this game . . . I'll read the instructions. (Jeanine read the instructions carefully and sorted out all the pieces. She seemed animated.)
J   I've never played this game before, have you?
T   No. We can learn a new game together. Do you and your mother play games sometimes?
J   No (frowning and concentrating on next move).
T   Would you like to?
J   I don't know (shrugged); she's always in her room anyway; let's play something else. (Jeanine neatly put away the game in exactly the same place from which she had removed it.)

Clinical Impressions: It was clear from witnessing Jeanine's play and playing the game with her that she was quite concerned with making order out of her world. She was willing to a small degree to engage the therapist, but it was the therapist who was supposed to "talk." She indicated a desire to relate more to the therapist by suggesting a highly structured interactive game that she chose and set up. Jeanine's need to be in control of the interaction was clear. As soon as she revealed information about her mother, she wanted to stop playing the game, a clear signal that she was feeling vulnerable.

What she did share indicated that she was lonely, that she felt alienated from her mother, and that she felt that her feelings did not count to her mother. Given her physical assaults on her mother, Jeanine may have felt unprotected and abandoned by her during the times of physical and sexual abuse. It was also clear that Jeanine was much younger than 13 years on a social level. She played more like a 10-year-old.

Later sessions progressed similarly: Jeanine was allowed to choose how she wanted to play, and the therapist and Jeanine began to discuss more of what Jeanine's life at home was like for her. At one point, Jeanine confessed that she wanted to be an architect and asked the therapist if she could design a house for her. Jeanine's fascination with ordering the world around her, especially houses, demonstrated her need to make her "house" different from what it had been. Jeanine was given much praise for her drawing talents and reassurance that she indeed could "design" her life better as she grew older. After a few sessions, Jeanine volunteered to complete her biography.

❑ Activity #2: Self-Portrait

Objective: To assess how the teen views him- or herself.

This activity is designed to help you assess how the teen sees him-or herself and to help in the assessment of the level of emotional maturity. Often, traumatized children's or adolescents' pictures depict a regressed image.

Malchiodi (1990) discussed commonalities in the artwork of abused children in her book *Breaking the Silence: Art Therapy With Children From Violent Homes.* These include sexual connotation, heads without bodies or bodies without the lower half, disorganization of body parts, encapsulation of a person, use of the color red and use of a complementary color scheme, use of heart-shaped imagery, artistic regression, use of circles and wedges, and self-deprecation. Her study focused on children in women's shelters who had been sexually abused.

In her work with abused children, Gil (1992) cited several observations of drawings by abused children: startled eyes, open mouth, displacement of parts of the body, layering of colors (not just shading), body encased in something, signs of injury ("symbol of injury"), open cavities, and splitting or dissociation (e.g., pictures of the child's "spirit" leaving the body).

Other observations regarding human figure drawings include the following: A small figure in relation to the size of the page may indicate low self-esteem; the degree of sexual differentiation may be related to sexual identity or developmental level; a sexualized-looking figure may reflect a tendency toward oversexualization; and missing legs, feet, or hands may reflect feelings of helplessness or passivity (Simonds, 1994). Simonds (1994) and Cantlay (1996) both noted that drawings with only heads and no bodies may signify sexual or physical abuse.

According to a study specific to adolescents in psychiatric hospital settings, wedge shapes, enclosed circles, and phallic-looking objects were found to be statistically significant indicators of sexual abuse (Sidun & Rosenthal, 1987).

We caution therapists who discover any of the above items to view these only as suggestive of possible abuse. An evaluation should always be done if there is a suspicion of abuse. We have also found it valuable to use the services of a certified art therapist whenever possible.

Ages: This activity is designed for children and adolescents of all ages. The younger or more emotionally immature or damaged adolescent will provide fewer details.

Materials Needed: Activity sheet and pencils, crayons, and/or markers.

Instructions: Instruct the adolescent to draw a picture of him- or herself that is as complete as possible. You may need to provide encouragement or ask questions to facilitate this activity. For example, let the teen know that he or she is not being judged on artistic ability. You might want to inquire whether there is more that he or she wants to include. Refrain from pointing out missing details or telling the teen what to include in the self-portrait, as these will become your indicators of how the adolescent views him- or herself.

Note: Regardless of the individual's age, concepts and feelings associated with the body may be uncomfortable or unpleasant if he or she has been sexually or physically abused. Therefore, there may be hesitation to engage in this activity, or the individual may give a regressed, impoverished version to comply minimally with the task.

It is important for you to make a mental note of various aspects of the self-portrait, but this will be explored in further detail in later chapters. This first exercise of the self-portrait is to assess how the teen sees him- or herself as the journey toward recovery is started.

Processing: If there is resistance, a little finesse may be needed to assist in processing this activity.

After the drawing is completed, ask the teen to tell you about the drawing. It is important to follow-up with queries to stimulate discussion (Karp & Butler, 1996; Simonds, 1994):

- Tell me about your picture.
- What seems interesting or unusual to you?
- How do you think you feel about yourself in your portrait?
- What is your mood here?
- How old do you look?
- Do you think anything is missing? What?
- What is the most important thing to you in this picture? Why?
- What do you like/dislike about yourself in your picture?

For a variation on this activity, you might also ask the teen to tell a story about the person in the picture.

The following case example will illustrate how one sexually, physically, and emotionally abused adolescent processed this activity.

Case Example: *Tina*

Brief Case History: Tina was a 15-year-old Caucasian teen admitted to an adolescent residential treatment center (RTC) from out of state for frequent runaway behavior, AOD abuse, and physical assaultiveness toward younger siblings. Tina had a history of emotional and physical abuse by her biological father. She alleged that about 1 month before her RTC admission, she had been raped by her

17-year-old boyfriend, Derek. She described Derek as a "Satanist" and a "skinhead."

Derek had allegedly raped her in the basement of her home while her parents were upstairs. She recalled the metal points of his leather bracelet, collar, and boots pressing on her skin while he pushed her down on the floor. She decided not to tell her parents about the rape because they did not like Derek and because she felt they would not believe her. Tina complained bitterly about being in treatment because she thought she needed to be at home to protect the family from being physically attacked by Derek and his friends.

Tina's behavior in group thus far had ranged from silly to serious, and she displayed frequent mood swings in a short period of time. She frequently engaged in word games with her peers and therapist to avoid focusing on her trauma.

Tina was given the instructions for Activity #2, which was to be completed during group therapy. She spent much more time than her peers on her self-portrait. She appeared to be devoting a great deal of effort to her drawing in that she was applying a lot of pressure with her marker and appeared very intent. She reluctantly finished it. The following dialogue ensued:

Therapist: Tina, would you tell the group about your self-portrait?

Tina (In an annoyed tone of voice) Do I have to? You can see what it is! (Tina displayed a rather bizarre drawing of what looked to be a gargoyle-like figure.)

Th That's true. We can see it, but we would like to hear how you see it.

T Okay. It's a guy. . . . Is that all right?

Th Whatever you draw is all right.

T Okay. Well, it's a gargoyle! It's ugly, it's mean!

Th Is that how you see yourself?

T (Laughing) It's really my father!

Th So, your self-portrait and your father are the same?

T Well, yeah. . . . That's what I said!

Th How do *you* feel in that picture?

T Pissed off!

The rest of the group session focused on peers' drawings.

Clinical Impression: Tina's view of herself is identified with her father—his anger and aggressiveness. Her anger is "male" and separate from herself. Making the self-portrait "male" shows her disconnection from her own anger as a female. She drew the angry self to be as ugly as possible. Tina has learned to see the emotion of anger (as demonstrated by father and Derek) as destructive, cruel, and ugly.

It appears that Tina still needs to keep her own anger separate from herself precisely because it is so destructive. However, this allows Tina to be sarcastic and passive-aggressive rather than in touch with and assertive with her anger (and perhaps other feelings as well). Fear of her own anger might lead to further victimization and further outbursts of rage, resulting in either danger to self or danger to others. Tina's work in treatment needs to focus on allowing herself to be actively and assertively angry. Comparisons to any future self-portraits could prove illuminating in charting her progress.

❏ Activity #3: My Family

Objective: To assist the teen in seeing him- or herself in relation to the family.

This activity is designed to assess how the adolescent views his or her family and how he or she fits into it. Again, you will be able to make an assessment regarding emotional maturity from the picture, as well as from the people who are included as part of the family unit.

Kaufman and Wohl (1992) aptly stated, "The family as an interactive system is more powerful than the total individual members. The family is a dynamic force that influences the growth and development of the offspring" (p. 29). Through this process, the child's identification of the self emerges as a result of the internalization of the parental figures' feelings and values. Consequently, if positive feelings and values are present, the child will most likely develop a healthy, positive self-image. If negative values and feelings are consistently experienced, the child may develop an unhealthy, negative self-image, which may persist into adolescence.

A great deal of information regarding the teen's perceptions of the family and his or her involvement with the family may be reflected in this activity. The teen may include additional people not normally included in the family, such as boyfriends, girlfriends, pets, and extended family. Conversely, the teen may elect to exclude people who normally would be included, such as him- or herself or other immediate family members.

The family drawing may elicit many different feelings, as outlined previously. It is important not to pressure the teen to include or exclude various people. It is possible that the teen may choose not to draw his or her family at all. Remember that the purpose of this activity is to build rapport and gather information. Therefore, it is important not to pressure the teen to complete the activity but rather to use the resistance as an opportunity to explore.

Ages: Adolescents aged 13 through 18 years should be able to complete this activity. The anxious or emotionally regressed teen may use stick figures.

Materials Needed: Activity sheet and pencils, crayons, markers, and/or colored pencils.

Instructions: Instruct the teen to draw a picture of his or her family.

Note: The teen who is no longer living with his or her biological family may need more assistance in terms of determining whom he or she considers "family." If he or she asks whom to include in the family drawing, a discussion of what "family" means to the teen may be necessary. It is important not to suggest whom the family should include.

Processing: After the family drawing is completed, it is helpful to ask about the people who were drawn. Make sure to label who everyone is. We have also found it beneficial to ask how each person in the picture is feeling. This gives you more insight into how the teen views the family dynamics.

Various pets in the family may be included. The more detail provided, the more you can learn about the family. Remember, this is a continuation of the rapport-building phase of recovery. As stated previously, do not pressure the teen if he or she does not want to elaborate on the drawing.

We have found that teens in general enjoy this activity. However, some have found it a difficult task, especially if they have been removed from their birth family.

Illustration 2.2 demonstrates how fragmented one teen saw her family as being. She drew her family as a jigsaw puzzle and drew two members as tombstones to indicate that they were dead (which was true).

❑ Activity #4: Family Activity

Objective: To assess how the teen's family interacts in a family activity.

This activity is designed not only to assess how the teen sees him- or herself in the family but to assess how the teen views interactions between family members.

Kaufman and Wohl (1992, pp. 99-126) described important aspects of the use of the kinetic family drawing (KFD) in work with abused children. They pointed out that the separation-individuation problem inherent in incestuous families may be reflected in the drawings of incest survivors. The members of the incestuous family are often enmeshed with each other in unhealthy ways that make the normal process of becoming more independent very difficult. This may be reflected in the drawings by the figures' stereotypic similarities, such as their all being the same height regardless of age or all wearing the same clothes. There is a lack of boundaries between family members.

Family coalitions, alliances, and disharmonies may also be revealed in the KFD. In the incestuous family, collusion is always present to some degree. In drawings this may be portrayed by compartmentalization, for example, the positioning of various family members as isolated or distanced from others. Other factors to consider include omission or inclusion of members of the family, erasures, shading, transparencies, and line quality (Kaufman & Wohl, 1992, p. 31).

This activity is not designed to assess the degree of damage or to determine whether abuse has occurred. It is included as part of the rapport-building process. Therefore, if you desire further information on this as an assessment technique, we recommend reviewing Kaufman and Wohl's (1992) book, as well as Malchiodi's (1990) book on using art therapy with abused children.

Art therapy is a specialized form of therapy that requires an advanced degree in art therapy. It may be useful to enlist the services of an art therapist if you desire a thorough interpretation of the artwork.

Ages: This activity is designed for adolescents aged 13 through 18 years. The anxious or emotionally regressed teen may include little detail or may use stick figures. Again, you may need to discuss who is included in the family (biological family, foster family, etc.).

Materials Needed: Activity sheet and pencils, crayons, markers, and/or colored pencils.

Instructions: Instruct the teen to draw his or her family doing something together.

Note: Be sure the teen includes him- or herself in the drawing. It is important to see how the teen sees the family interactions. It is a statement of how the teen perceives him- or herself in the family setting and how the teen views the family interactions (Kaufman & Wohl, 1992).

Processing: After the picture is completed, engage the teen in conversation about what the family is doing. We have found it helpful to ask how old he or she is in the picture. If the teen experienced early childhood abuse, removal from the birth family, or has experienced the death of a parent, he or she may put him- or herself in the picture as a child or baby.

As stated for the previous activity, it is also helpful to ask about how each family member feels while doing the activity drawn in the picture.

❑ **Activity #5: My Three Wishes**

Objective: To allow the individual to explore his or her wishes in life.

This activity is designed to have abused teens explore magical thinking in terms of how they would handle complete power over their life. This activity will help in the assessment of how fragile the teen may be.

The healthier teen with better ego strength is likely to list three wishes that reflect a sense of realistic hope for the future, such as wanting to go to college. If the teen continues to struggle with an overwhelming sense of pain, the three wishes may be unrealistic or may reflect his or her sense of helplessness, as in "I wish I could just die or go away forever." The teen may also react to this activity with statements such as "Why wish for anything—I never get what I want anyway." This kind of remark could provide the basis for a fruitful discussion of the teen's sense of deprivation.

Ages: This activity is designed for teens aged 13 through 18 years.

Materials Needed: Activity sheet and pencils.

Instructions: Instruct the teen to think for a moment about his or her three most important wishes. Then ask, "If you could have any three wishes in the world, what would they be?" Then instruct the teen to write down the three wishes.

Processing: After the teen has revealed his or her three wishes, we have found it very informative to ask such questions as "Which is the most important wish?" "How do you feel about each wish?" and "If you could change a wish, which one would you change?"

❑ **Activity #6: Reflections of Myself**

Objective: To enable the teen to see him- or herself from a different perspective by viewing his or her reflection in a mirror.

This activity is designed to assess how the adolescent sees him- or herself from a different perspective. This allows the teen to be a bit more objective in that he or she is encouraged to focus on details observed in a mirror. Since most teens (especially girls) spend a great deal of time in front of the mirror, this activity can be interesting. The teen who suffers from an eating disorder may find this activity very difficult. However, it can be very informative to the therapist.

Ages: This activity is designed for adolescents without severe developmental delays or intellectual deficits. The individual must be able to transfer images that he or she sees onto paper. This activity is rather abstract.

Materials Needed: Activity sheet, large mirror or hand-held mirror, and crayons, pencils, markers, and/or colored pencils.

Instructions: Instruct the teen to look in a mirror and to study his or her face for a minute or two. Then ask the teen to write about the reflection in the mirror. For those with developmental delays or for those who are intellectually challenged, it may be easier to draw what they see.

Processing: After the activity is completed, we have found it helpful to follow up with questions about what the teen sees when looking in the mirror, what feelings he or she sees in the picture, and how the picture in the mirror differs from the image of him- or herself in the mind. It is also informative to ask how it felt to write about or draw the image as opposed to just a self-portrait from memory.

❏ **Activity #7: Self-Collage**

Objective: To encourage self-expression in a fun and creative way by making a collage.

This activity is designed to allow the adolescent to express him-or herself in another modality. Making collages is a common activity for many teens. It is less threatening because they can cut and paste materials that are already created. Many abused individuals have such low self-esteem that drawing can be intimidating because they are afraid of being judged. It is interesting to see what is chosen as a representation of the self.

Ages: This activity is designed for children or adolescents of all ages. However, if the individual is developmentally or intellectually challenged, the concept of this activity may not be understood as readily, and a simple instruction to choose items that he or she likes may suffice.

Materials Needed: Activity sheet, a variety of magazines and/or pictures that can be cut up, a large sheet of paper, glue, and scissors.

Instructions: Instruct the individual to sit at a table and think about him- or herself. Explain that while the individual is looking through the materials, he or she may cut out any words, phrases, or pictures that reflect the self. When he or she is finished, the next step is to arrange the pictures on the large sheet of paper and glue them down in any way he or she chooses.

Many teens may ask, "What do you mean when you say 'myself'—do you mean how I see myself or how other people see me?" This may be best answered by reflecting their question back and asking what would mean more to them.

Processing: After the collage is completed, we have found it helpful to ask the teen to tell you about the collage. It can be informative to go over each object on the collage and have him or her tell you about how each one of the objects or pictures reflects him- or herself. It is also useful to ask which object is liked the most and which the least, and why. If it becomes obvious that the teen made the collage from the viewpoint of how others see him or her, then this needs to be explored further.

❑ **Activity #8: I Like Me Because . . .**

Objective: To allow the adolescent to explore various positive things about him- or herself.

This activity is designed not only to begin recognizing and verbalizing positive statements about the self but to assess the adolescent's feelings of self-worth. Abused children and adolescents tend to have a damaged view of self. Building self-esteem becomes an important therapy goal.

Ages: This activity is designed for children and adolescents of all ages. The developmentally delayed or intellectually challenged adolescent may need assistance with writing or spelling. Regardless of their age, adolescents with significantly low self-esteem may need a great deal of encouragement and prompting to complete this activity.

Materials Needed: Activity sheet and pencils, colored pencils, crayons, and/or markers.

Instructions: Instruct the teen to write at least five things that he or she likes about him- or herself.

Note: If the teen has difficulty naming attributes, be encouraging by pointing out several positive qualities you have observed.

Teens with significantly low self-esteem may have a difficult time identifying five things they like about themselves. They may identify things not really connected with themselves but rather a part of their world, such as "I like my Walkman, my CDs, my dog; I like to talk to guys and smoke cigarettes." This is acceptable at this stage of the recovery process because it reflects something about themselves, even if not very deep. It is important not to be judgmental at this stage in the recovery process.

Processing: After the activity is completed, we have found it very helpful to process each statement by asking about each positive attribute. It is informative to ask which positive attribute is valued the most and why, as well as any feelings the teen had while completing this activity.

❏ Activity #9: My Goals

Objective: To encourage the adolescent to set goals regarding what he or she wants to accomplish in therapy.

This activity is designed to assist the teen in beginning to share "therapeutic goals" in a nonthreatening manner. Most abused children and adolescents have a difficult time organizing thoughts and feelings, let alone setting goals.

It is important for abused teens to learn goal setting so they can move from being victims to being survivors. As a victim, the child or adolescent has been placed in a vulnerable position of being powerless, learning a sense of helplessness. For healing to take place, there must be movement from a position of powerlessness to a position of healthy empowerment.

This activity will assist in creating movement toward a sense of empowerment by allowing the teen to set goals in a nonthreatening way. This can be accomplished by first thinking about behaviors and attitudes that are identified as problem areas. Changing these can become the therapeutic goals.

Ages: This activity is designed for adolescents of all ages. Even developmentally delayed or intellectually challenged teens should be able to list things they want to work on. The teen with writing difficulties may need to dictate his or her responses to you. The resistant teen may need your assistance in processing nonthreatening goals at this stage in the therapy to complete this activity.

Materials Needed: Activity sheet and pencils, crayons, colored pencils, and/or markers.

Instructions: Instruct the teen to think of the behaviors and attitudes he or she would like to change about him-or herself. Then have the teen write five things he or she would like to change about him- or herself. Hopefully, these will become guides for therapeutic goals.

Note: It will be important to assist the teen to stay focused on changes in the "self" rather than changes in others, such as "I would like my mother to be nicer and quit hitting me."

Processing: After the activity is completed, we have found it important to follow up with various questions about what changes the teen would like to have happen, which change is the most important, and how the teen can make these changes happen. It is also informative to check out the feelings about these changes and whether the teen feels that the changes are possible.

3

Feelings

Feelings are the reactions that occur within individuals as they respond to the world and to stimuli inside and outside themselves. Feelings or emotions can be affected by what people think, see, hear, touch, smell, and taste.

Many times people who have been abused learn to "stuff" their feelings or emotions. Suppressing feelings becomes another unhealthy coping mechanism. Abused children and adolescents may use this technique as a way to keep their secret, pretend nothing has happened, and protect or care for themselves when the adults around them are not keeping them safe. All too often, individuals who have been abused have had their feelings and emotions invalidated by others; such invalidation is yet another way they learn to stuff their feelings.

These adolescents need to learn that everyone has feelings and that it is healthy and normal to feel a variety of feelings. They also need to develop an understanding that it is acceptable to experience any feeling. They need to view feelings as "comfortable" or "uncomfortable" rather than "good" or "bad." Finally, they need to understand that feelings or emotions can be triggered by different situations and that people respond in different ways.

The goal of this chapter is to aid teens in identifying various feelings. These feelings may be associated directly with the abuse or with the lasting effects of abusive experiences. In addition, the goal includes helping adolescents learn how to communicate feelings so that they are more able to control the feelings as opposed to letting the feelings control them. The ability to communicate feelings and emotions is a vital piece of the abused teen's recovery and an essential skill in becoming a survivor.

The activities in this chapter are designed to assist adolescents in identifying, confronting, and expressing various feelings that may be associated with their abuse history. As individuals begin to get in touch with feelings in general, they may become overwhelmed by a flood of feelings that have been repressed. The therapist needs to be prepared for unpredictable reactions by the teen.

Reactions to addressing abusive experiences may include an escalation in problematic behaviors such as aggression, self-abusive behaviors, alcohol or other drug abuse, sexual acting out, prostitution, gang-related identification or behaviors, decline in school performance, significant changes in peer group identification, and other rule-violating behaviors.

It is important for all those who work with the abused teen to be prepared for the possibility of acting out. Therefore, providing structure is an important component in helping everyone involved in the teen's treatment to feel a sense of safety. Again, this goes back to having firmly established a strong therapeutic alliance so that the teen has a sense of trust and security, which is necessary as he or she begins to confront difficult feelings.

This may be a time when the family needs to be included in family therapy as part of the teen's treatment plan. The family system will be affected by the teen's reaction to individual therapy. Therefore, it is important to address therapy's impact on the family unit.

As in the previous chapter, this chapter includes a few case studies to illustrate how some of the activities presented have been used in actual therapy situations. We have given a brief case history, an example of dialogue between the therapist and the teen during the activity, and clinical impressions. We have also provided a section called "Processing" at the end of each of the activity descriptions because it is important to engage in thorough processing of thoughts and feelings as the teen moves forward in his or her trauma resolution work. As you found in the last chapter, the suggestions for processing are general, and you will most likely add your own ideas as you get to know the teen.

Prior to working on the activities in this chapter, you may want to read the section "Teen Talk" in the *Activity Book* to familiarize yourself with how the topic of feelings is introduced to the teen. In addition, you will want to instruct the teen to read the "Teen Talk" section in his or her *Activity Book* before beginning the activities in this chapter.

❏ **Activity #10: How Would You Feel?**

Objective: To be able to express feelings associated with given life experiences depicted in various vignettes.

This activity is designed to assist the teen in moving from simply labeling feelings to matching his or her own feelings with the given life experiences depicted in the vignettes. This activity may begin to increase the anxiety level as feelings are elicited. It is important for the teen to begin differentiating between "comfortable" and "uncomfortable" feelings, as opposed to "good" and "bad" feelings.

Ages: Adolescents between the ages of 13 and 18 years should be able to complete this activity with little difficulty if they can read; if they cannot, the vignettes can be read to them. The given situations are on a concrete, simple level.

Materials Needed: Activity sheet and pencils, crayons, colored pencils, and/or markers.

Instructions: Instruct the teen to read each vignette (this can be done alone or with your help). After he or she has read the vignette, have him or her write about his or her feelings associated with the given situation.

Processing: After the activity is completed, we have found it helpful to go over each vignette and ask questions, such as "How would you feel in this situation?" "Tell me about a similar experience you had," "Which situation makes you feel most comfortable?" and "Which situation makes you feel most uncomfortable?"

❏ **Activity #11: My Feelings**

Objective: To learn how to identify and share feelings using "I feel" statements.

This activity is designed to assist adolescents in developing a healthy way to express feelings so that they can better get their needs met. While they are working on this activity, they are encouraged to use a variety of "feeling" words to broaden their range of expression.

Ages: Teens of all ages should be able to complete this activity. If they have reading or writing difficulties, you can read the statements aloud, and the teen can dictate the response.

Materials Needed: Activity sheet and pencil.

Instructions: Instruct the individual to complete the "I feel" statements.

Processing: After the statements are completed, have the teen read his or her responses, and discuss how they can apply this process to real life situations.

❏ **Activity #12: Feelings Charade**

Objective: To enable teens to practice the nonverbal expression of their feelings in order to promote their self-awareness, to help them learn how accurately they are able to express themselves, and to increase their ability to "read" others nonverbally. This activity is a beginning step in becoming more assertive.

Although traumatized teens may experience many emotions, they may not be aware of how, if at all, they are expressing these emotions to others. This exercise allows them to focus on very specific feelings (ranging from the obvious to the more subtle) and to try to get the feeling across to others without using words. Encourage the teen to exaggerate; a helper may be chosen from group to whisper suggestions if necessary. This is a particularly revealing exercise for those teens who complain, "I don't know how I feel" or "I'm confused."

Many traumatized individuals have no difficulty at all in reading others' emotions because they learned early the importance of this survival skill. If your group is particularly successful with this part of the exercise, you can have a discussion focused on this valuable skill and how it can help them in the future (in a healthier way, of course).

Ages: Adolescents between the ages of 13 and 18 years should be able to do this exercise. Some may balk because they are afraid of being judged; assure them that there is no "right" or "wrong" way to do this activity and that it might be fun.

Materials Needed: Prepare a handout for each group member consisting of a list of 20 feelings (see *Activity Manual*). Write each feeling on a 3-by-5 card and divide the cards into three sets, as instructed in the *Activity Book*, according to whether the emotions are simple/easy to portray, more complex/harder to portray, or very complex/hardest to portray. This activity is adapted from Pearl Berman's *Therapeutic Exercises for Victimized and Neglected Girls* (1994).

Instructions: Give out the list to all group members except the "actor." Give the actor Set #1 ("easiest to portray"). The "actor" chooses what to act out nonverbally. The rest of the group guesses from the list what feeling is being portrayed (encourage peers to study the actor and not to randomly guess). Depending on how many teens are in the group, decide how many cards each peer will receive. Go on to Sets #2 (harder to portray) and #3 (hardest to portray). In individual therapy, the therapist and the teen can take turns.

Note: This activity can also be used successfully in family therapy to facilitate communication between family members and to increase awareness of how much may be expressed nonverbally in the home.

Processing: How teens respond to this activity, whether with enthusiasm or resistance, and how well they convey and read feelings can help you, the therapist, in assessing important areas of strengths and weaknesses. If teens are not able to demonstrate particular feelings or to read them, this deficiency will require special attention. They will have difficulty letting others know about their needs and will not be able to pick up on the subtleties of possibly unsafe situations. Being comfortable in the world of emotions can be very problematic for many trauma victims due to the damage to the sense of self. Peers may guess rather than seriously consider what is being acted out, and the "actor" may struggle with the portrayal of such emotions as "secure" or "content."

This activity provides the opportunity for peers to give each other feedback and for the therapist to ask questions about how feelings have been expressed in the family: For example, "How do you know when someone in your family is happy/upset?" "What feeling was the easiest/hardest to show here in the group/with me?" "What feeling was the easiest/hardest to show with your family?" This discussion can also lead into how individuals felt when they were being victimized and how they took care of themselves. If it is appropriate, the therapist can explain common defenses such as rationalization, minimization, and denial, as well as how dissociation works.

❑ Activity #13: Feelings Collage

Objective: To focus on feelings by identifying different pictures, phrases, and/or words that reflect various experiences.

This activity is designed to encourage the adolescent to express him- or herself in a relatively nonthreatening manner. It is interesting to see what adolescents choose as representations of their feelings when looking through magazines or pictures.

Ages: Teens of all ages should be able to complete this activity with limited assistance.

Materials Needed: A variety of magazines and/or pictures that can be cut up, a large sheet of paper, glue, and scissors.

Instructions: Instruct the teen to sit quietly at a table and reflect on his or her feelings and experiences. As the teen looks through the magazines and/or pictures, he or she should keep in mind the feelings to be portrayed in the collage. Tell the individual that he or she may cut out any words, phrases, or pictures. Encourage the teen to keep cutting until he or she feels finished. Then the various pictures, words, and phrases should be arranged on a large sheet of paper and glued down.

Processing: After the collage is completed, it is important to process the collage by engaging the teen with queries such as "Tell me about your collage," "Tell me about the different feelings expressed in your collage," "What's the most important part of your collage? Why?" and "Did you leave anything out? What?"

❑ **Activity #14: Feelings Mask**

Objective: To explore how the teen feels inside and how he or she presents him- or herself to others.

This activity is designed to encourage the individual to explore his or her feelings and how these feelings are manifested on the "outside." The teen may find that the feelings expressed outwardly are very different from what is felt on the "inside." Teenagers are very good at "masking" their feelings; therefore, this activity should challenge them to identify this dynamic. Hopefully, they will begin to reveal deeper feelings that they hide from others.

Ages: Adolescents of all ages should find this to be a challenging yet fun activity.

Materials Needed: Two paper plates, stapler or glue, popsicle sticks or tongue depressors, and crayons, markers, colored pencils, and/ or paints.

Instructions: Instruct the teen to sit at a table and take two paper plates. Have the teen draw on one of the paper plates how he or she feels most of the time on the "inside."

Next, ask the teen how others see him or her on the "outside" and to draw that expression on the other paper plate. Then instruct the individual to either staple or glue the backs of the plates together. Instruct him or her to be sure to place the stick between the plates before securing them together.

Processing: After the mask is completed, it is important to process the activity with queries such as "Tell me about the feelings you have drawn on your plates," "Which one is how you feel in the inside? Why?" "Which one is how other people see you? Why?" and (if the two feelings are different) "What makes it difficult to show your inside feelings to others?" Have the teen hold up the feelings mask in front of his or her face to experience more vividly the contrast between the inner experience and the outer presentation.

Case Example: *Trevor*

Brief Case History: Trevor was a 16-year-old African American male whose mother had brought him to an outpatient trauma recovery group for adolescent boys after he had run away twice. He was frequently truant from school and had been suspended once for fighting. Trevor had also shoplifted and had refused to bring the item back to the store when his mother discovered it. His mother explained that these behaviors had started getting worse about 6 months ago, although she had been worried about him for at least a year. Trevor's parents had been separated for many months but were now considering reconciling. The mother described the relationship as having been "very stormy" and thought that things were now much better. She thought it was possible that Trevor had been "traumatized" by the separation. Trevor did not want to say much about his father when his mother was present.

Later, when he was alone with the therapist in the intake session, he revealed that his father used to hit both him and his mother. Trevor described much emotional as well as physical abuse. The father seemed to enjoy humiliating Trevor by denigrating his masculine identity and telling him he was acting like a "girl" or a "fag" if he did anything less than perfectly. One time he sprayed Trevor with the garden hose in front of neighborhood kids, calling Trevor a "sissy." Trevor described getting very angry at this treatment, especially when he was younger. He eventually realized that his father wanted him to get mad so he could have an excuse to hit him. As he got older, Trevor began to avoid being home any chance he could. He had been happy and relieved when his mother finally threw her husband out, but now he could not bear the thought that the father might be returning to the home. He said that he had tried to explain all these things to his mother but that "she just doesn't seem to get that he's only acting nice so he can come back." Trevor was obviously acting out his anger and upset, but he was hurting himself in the process and then blaming his father.

The following is an example of a dialogue between Trevor, his peers, and the therapist after completing the above activity:

Therapist Trevor, it's your turn to show us your mask.

Trevor I'd really rather not; it looks dumb.

Peer Come on, Trevor, we showed you our masks!

T Yeah, but you guys did a good job; I can't draw right. . . . (Looking down at the floor)

Th Let's remember the point of the activity is to show if how we feel inside is different than what we show the world. It's not a drawing contest. I bet your mask is quite interesting, Trevor.

T Can't I show it to you alone?

Th What are you concerned about?

T That everyone will think I'm dumb.

Th Like your father did?

T Yeah. . . . I mean, I know you guys aren't going to make fun of me, but I still get this scared feeling inside. . . .

Peer It wasn't easy for me either—maybe you could just show us one side and we could guess if it's your inside or your outside.

T Well, okay. . . . (holds up the side showing a mean, angry face)

Th Hmm. . . . You know, I'm not sure which part of you that is. Sometimes you act really angry, and other times you seem rather shy. . . .

T That's how I act to the world! I'm angry all the time!

Clinical Impressions: Of course, Trevor still felt hurt and angry from his father's maltreatment of him and of his mother. But he was also using his anger as a defense to hide behind. When he let his guard down, Trevor behaved as if he had no self-confidence at all. He had no idea how to behave "in between"; he had to either be angry or be a total wimp. These were the only two options for being a "man" that his father had given him.

Although his mother had demonstrated strength in separating from her husband, Trevor now saw her as a "wimp" for considering reconciling. In terms of relationships with the opposite sex, one might imagine Trevor getting involved with a domineering young woman in an effort to find a "strong" female or perhaps, at the other extreme, finding a very passive female whom he could dominate himself. In reality, Trevor saw himself as a "loser" when it came to girls, having internalized his father's opinion of him.

Except for brief acting-out episodes, Trevor actually behaved more like the sad, lonely, humiliated young man on the other side of his mask. Because Trevor intellectually rejected the values his father embodied, he was afraid of his own anger; he scared himself every time he got "in trouble." Trevor needed to work in therapy sessions on expressing his anger toward both his father and his mother.

Hopefully, gaining mastery in this arena of feelings would buoy his self-esteem. Hearing positive feedback from his male peers and the male co-therapist might also help him to think better of himself. In addition, Trevor had to work on self-protection skills in case his father did return to the home unchanged. Trevor's mother would also benefit from individual therapy to work on her ambivalent attachment to Trevor. Trevor was asked to give some thought to living with his aunt and uncle, who presented a much healthier relationship.

In addition, Trevor had to work on self-protection skills in case his father did return to the home unchanged. Trevor's mother would also benefit from individual therapy to work on her ambivalent attachment to Trevor. Trevor was asked to give some thought to living with his aunt and uncle, who present a much healthier relationship.

Trevor could be at high risk to become a batterer like his father. According to Dutton (1995), exposure to a father's shaming behavior, the father's abuse of the mother, and an ambivalent attachment to the mother all contribute the creation of the cyclically assaultive man. Trevor's history is in accordance with this profile. Therefore, it is crucial for the therapist to take note of any such warning signs and to plan treatment accordingly.

❏ **Activity #15: Scrapbook of Feelings**

Objective: To have the adolescent express feelings by organizing in a scrapbook items that represent feelings associated with significant life experiences.

This activity is designed to teach the adolescent how to evaluate and organize important feelings he or she may have felt with regard to different experiences over time. This book can be organized by separate sections for different feelings, chronologically, or by events. This activity is designed to take place over a long period of time. It may be an ongoing activity that is done alongside other activities.

Ages: Adolescents from 13 to 18 years should be able to begin this project with little assistance.

Materials Needed: Buy a scrapbook or make your own. Have available magazines; other pictures; glue; crayons, markers, and/or colored pencils; and scissors. It is important to have teens bring in various items that represent various feelings they have experienced for inclusion in the scrapbook.

Instructions: Instruct the teen to begin collecting various items, magazine pictures, phrases, photographs, and so forth that have meaning and/or represent feelings he or she has experienced. Help the teen decide how to organize the scrapbook (e.g., by feelings, time frames, or events). Then instruct the teen to begin putting the items on paper in the scrapbook. This is a project that may take some time to complete. Allow the teen to be as creative as he or she desires.

Note: The teen may want to take the scrapbook home and work on his or her own. If there is a problem with privacy at home, it may be best to leave the scrapbook with the therapist.

Processing: After the scrapbook is completed, a session should be set aside to go through the entire scrapbook, and the items should be processed. It may be helpful to give prompts such as "Tell me about the items you have collected," "Tell me about the feelings each one represents. Why?" and "How does it feel to complete this project?"

❏ Activity #16: Feelings Essay

Objective: To assess the progress the adolescent has made in learning how to accurately identify and appropriately express his or her feelings.

This activity gives both the teen and the therapist a chance to gauge the extent to which the teen has been able to process his or her deeper feelings. It may now be obvious which defenses are used by the teen as coping strategies.

Ages: Teens from 13 to 18 years should be able to complete this activity. The level of sophistication of the essay will depend on the teen's developmental maturity.

Materials Needed: Activity sheet, pencils or pens, and crayons, colored pencils, and/or markers.

Instructions: Have the teen sit and think about a feeling that stood out as he or she worked on the activities in this chapter. The teen can refer to the feelings listed in Activity #11 if needed. Then have the teen write about any feeling he or she wishes. Also allow him or her to add a drawing if desired.

Processing: Have the teen read the essay aloud and process feelings associated with it. If this takes place in a group setting, peers can give feedback.

Case Example: *Karla "Night Star"*

Brief Case History: Karla, whose Native American name is "Night Star," was a 15-year-old referred for individual therapy by the juvenile court system following multiple arrests for a variety of crimes, including petty theft, burglary, assault, curfew violation, and affiliation with known gang members. When Karla initially entered therapy, she was living with her single mother, her 18-year-old sister (who was 3 months pregnant), the sister's 23-year-old boyfriend, and four younger sisters, ranging in age from 2 to 13 years old. Her family was living in a two-bedroom apartment in a low-income housing project that was known for its violent crimes and drug activity. After approximately 4 months, her mother left the family without notice, returning to the reservation. The children suspected that she had gone on another one of her drinking binges.

Though Karla was Native American, she identified with the Hispanic gang culture of her neighborhood. She was actively involved in a barrio gang and readily accepted the violent, substance-using and -abusing, and very sexually active lifestyle. All in all, developing rapport with Karla was very difficult. It took many sessions before she would answer or engage in even a superficial conversation. However, once she began to trust, she was able to share some of her past abusive experiences.

It was obvious that Karla had been neglected throughout her upbringing; her mother would frequently disappear on drinking binges, leaving the children to the care of the state, friends, or family. In addition, Karla was able to discuss some of the physical abuse she and her siblings had endured from her mother, mother's boyfriends, and other caregivers. The cycle of domestic violence was continuing in that her older sister's African American boyfriend was now attempting to take a "father figure" role. He verbally abused the children and frequently made threats of physical abuse. Karla had a very difficult time listening to this man because of his threats of violence and because she did not accept his ethnic background.

Although Karla did not discuss any sexual abuse history when she was younger, the therapist suspected that it had occurred. Karla did discuss her ongoing, very promiscuous sexual lifestyle, and she was able to discuss an incident of rape that she had suffered in the last year and a half.

Karla was asked to think of the three feelings she felt most of the time. Initially, she was somewhat resistant even to engage in the activity. However, once she was reassured that she would not have to describe her feelings in writing but could draw them instead, she let down her defenses.

Therapist Karla, I want you to think about the three feelings that you experience most of the time.

Karla I don't feel anything. I don't like to think about my feelings.

T I know it's difficult sometimes, but we all have feelings. And like we've talked about before, one of your challenges is to be able to express your feelings in healthier ways.

K Yeah, you're right.

T I'm not going to ask you to talk about your feelings. I just want you to think about the feelings you have and draw a picture of them, since you don't want to write about your feelings.

K What do you mean?

T Well, I want you to think about how you picture these feelings. You know, if you couldn't use words and you wanted to let someone know how you felt so you had to describe it through a drawing. Even though I know you would never want to do that! (both laughed)

K You're right there, Miss! Okay, I can do that. But instead of drawing one picture, can I just draw separate pictures?

T Sure, you can do this any way that works for you.

For the remainder of this session, Karla worked on her pictures; then we discussed them in the next session. The next excerpt was from the second session. Karla had drawn only one picture, and she said that was all she could do.

T   So, Karla, tell me about this picture.

K   Well I don't really know why I drew that. I just like these kind of flowers, don't you? Me and my home girls draw these, and someday I'm going to get a tattoo like this.

T   What feeling do you have when you look at this picture, or what feeling do you think other people see when they look at it?

K   I don't know. I guess when other people look at it they probably see sadness because of these things (pointed at the droplike figures coming off the petals).

T   I can see why you might say that—they kind of do remind me of teardrops.

The session continued with a discussion about the different events that had caused Karla a great deal of sadness.

Clinical Impressions: Because Karla was unwilling to complete the essay, she was encouraged to draw a picture reflecting her feelings. Her continued unwillingness was reflective of her oppositional and defiant style. She engaged in power struggles and therefore resisted the therapist's suggestion to write an essay. She was surrounded by abusive, authoritarian figures and saw the therapist as one more adult ordering her around. She was attempting to exercise her autonomy by this behavior. The therapist chose not to engage in the power struggle by allowing Karla to exercise power and control by completing the activity her way, which was to draw a picture depicting her feelings.

Part of the healing process is allowing the teen to gain a sense of empowerment. This requires the therapist to be flexible in designing or redesigning the activities. Engaging in a power struggle with the teen is futile and countertherapeutic.

In our experience, we have found the picture drawn by Karla to be a common motif in Hispanic popular art. This supports Karla's self-expressed identification with Hispanic culture. However, it is interesting to note that Karla signed the picture with her Native American name, Night Star. This reveals some confusion as to cultural identity. Karla described tears coming from the petals. This reflects the deeper sadness that Karla masks with anger and oppositional behavior.

Boundaries

Boundaries can be defined as limits or borders that can be experienced as physical, emotional, or sexual. People who have been abused have experienced a violation of their boundaries. Their sense of personal control in their world was taken away. They were left feeling powerless over their ability to protect their personal space. Often these individuals have not learned the right to privacy or the right to emotional distance and separateness due to their abusive experiences.

When a child or adolescent is beaten or sexually molested, it is fairly clear that his or her boundaries have been violated. But the less visible abuse, such as emotional or psychological abuse, is often ignored. Persons who have been verbally assaulted have also had their boundaries violated. The child who has been rejected, isolated, or undernurtured may be left confused as to what healthy or unhealthy boundaries are. For individuals who have undergone any of these experiences, boundary issues are significant.

Children and adolescents who have been abused have a diffuse sense of boundaries. They are uncertain and confused regarding the appropriateness of others' behavior toward them, as well as their behavior toward others. Many times, these victims become "reactive abusers" violating other people's personal space physically or emotionally. Sometimes this is a result of diffuse boundaries; other times it is a way to regain the sense of power and control lost in the original abuse.

In most families of abuse-reactive children, the parents have not provided a model of good boundary management for family members (Gil & Johnson, 1993). Appropriate boundary development is essential. Often, victims of abuse have been exposed to either no boundaries or "loose" boundaries in their home setting. Sexually, this could include the parent(s) and child bathing together, sleeping together on a regular basis, engaging in inappropriate kissing (tongue kissing), wearing questionable attire (often walking around with very little on), or sharing inappropriate sexual materials (videos, pictures, magazines, stories).

It is important that you, as a therapist, assess your own personal approach to maintaining appropriate boundaries. Though some therapists feel very comfortable hugging, this can be misinterpreted. However, providing nurturing remains an important part of the therapeutic process.

Briere (1992) aptly pointed out that the abuse survivor's dependence on the therapist is healthy. He suggested that this might be reframed as "attachment" rather than "dependency." Nurturing is necessary so that therapy-appropriate needs can be met. In addition, the adolescent must be encouraged in the process of individuation. Such encouragement includes communicating appropriate boundaries and providing support and validation.

In order to provide appropriate boundaries while still nurturing, the therapist may want to limit frontal hugging and switch to hugging from the side. This may be less stimulating to sexualized adolescents and less threatening to physically abused teens. Some therapists prefer to shake hands with the extremely sexualized adolescent who is seeking constant body contact.

The goal of this chapter is to assist the teen in understanding the importance of healthy boundaries as well as ways to establish them. The development of healthy boundaries is another important step in the recovery process.

The activities in this chapter are designed to assist teens in identifying, differentiating, and developing boundaries in their environment. Because abused adolescents' boundaries have been violated, the activities in this chapter may be very difficult for some to complete without experiencing a great deal of pain and anxiety and subsequently manifesting resistance. Patience, persistence, and understanding will be especially important at this stage in recovery.

Case studies are included in this chapter to assist you in further understanding of how some of these activities have been used in actual therapy situations. As in the preceding chapters, we have given a brief case history, an example of dialogue during the activity, and clinical impressions. We hope this helps you in your own work with abused adolescents.

"Sean's Story," provided in the *Activity Book* for this chapter, seems to provoke a lot of discussion in group therapy (see Activity #19). This is a time when some teens begin to self-disclose. They may relate to various aspects of the story and share their own experiences.

Although this chapter is still focused on the beginning stages of trauma recovery, some adolescents may trust enough to jump ahead. It is important to stay focused on the activity, while allowing them to relate feelings that stem from prior (or current) maltreatment.

The section "Teen Talk" in the *Activity Book* is a general introduction to the concept of boundaries. You will want to read this and have the adolescent read it before beginning the activities.

❏ Activity #17: Developing Boundaries—Stop!

Objective: To enable teens to learn experientially what their physical boundaries are in a safe environment. Teens will hopefully gain a sense of mastery as well.

This activity has been designed to allow peers in a group (or an individual in individual therapy) to physically experience setting limits as well as to learn to recognize and respond to their "inner voice." Children or adolescents who have been abused, whether physically, sexually, or emotionally, have had their boundaries and personal space violated.

Not only has someone entered that space without permission and hurt them, but frequently that person has told the child, "This is for your own good," "You deserve this," or "This hurts me more than it hurts you." These messages serve to further confuse the perception of the abused child as to what is right or wrong for him or her. Therefore, the teenager you are working with may not know how to recognize or interpret warning signs from the environment that could be providing valuable information about the need to protect oneself.

Many abused teens ignore their gut feelings about people and situations. This is a result of being put in the position of ignoring how they were really feeling when experiencing trauma earlier in life. They may have come to the conclusion that bad things happened to them and they felt bad afterwards because they were "bad" themselves. Often they do not view the abuser (particularly if the abuser had been a loved/trusted person in their lives) as the "bad" one. (This has been discussed in the introduction to this book as the "abuse dichotomy" described by Briere, 1992.) Therefore, having teens practice setting limits and respecting their own (and others') boundaries is very important for preventing revictimization and for helping teens to gain a sense of mastery in their lives.

Ages: Adolescents between the ages of 13 and 18 years should be able to do this activity. Some teens may feel self-conscious and act silly, but in our experience, once they do the exercise and feel more powerful, they enjoy themselves.

Materials Needed: Activity sheet and pencils. Depending on how many teens you are working with, you may need a larger room.

Instructions for Group: Instruct the teens to divide themselves into two separate lines facing each other and standing as far apart as possible. Each person should be able to look across the room at another person. If there is an odd number, the therapist can participate if that seems appropriate; if not, let a peer be the "observer" in order to give feedback (the activity can be done again so that the observer has a chance to participate). Tell the teens in one of the lines that they are to very slowly walk toward the person that they are facing. Instruct the other line that they are to put up their hand (palm facing the person walking toward them) and say "Stop!" at the moment they cease being comfortable with the space between them. The other person then has to stop immediately. Have the two lines switch roles and repeat.

A variation of this activity is to ask two of the teens to do this activity in front of the group after the entire group has had the opportunity of doing it once. These two teens can demonstrate how they would handle someone walking very quickly toward them or not respecting the "Stop!" signal. It would be best to choose two teens who would be appropriate role models for the others.

Instructions for Individual Therapy: The above instructions can be modified to include the therapist and teen as the two lines. It may be best to have the therapist be the one to say "Stop!" first to reduce anxiety for the teen. If you perceive that this will still be too threatening for the teen, puppets, stuffed toys, or dolls may be used. Then you can ask the teen how he or she thinks the puppet/toy/doll experienced the activity. If the teen is unwilling to participate at all, you may want to engage him or her in a general discussion of what he or she considers to be personal space; drawing may be a useful adjunct in this situation.

For immature or significantly regressed teens, you may even find some of the activities in Chapter 4 of *Treatment Strategies for Abused Children* (Karp & Butler, 1996) to be suitable.

Processing: This activity usually generates a lot of animated conversation, so it is important to help peers structure their responses. Responses to the questions should be written on their activity sheets first and then shared with the group.

The following case example will illustrate how one abused teenaged girl processed this activity.

Case Example: *Patrice*

Brief Case History: Patrice was a 16-year-old Navajo Indian girl sent to an adolescent treatment facility. She had been living with a foster family for the past 2 years in a large city in the same state. Patrice had a significant history of alcohol and drug abuse beginning at age 12 and was now making suicidal gestures, such as overdosing on aspirin.

Patrice had lived on the reservation with her mother, her two sisters, and her stepfather from birth to age 11. After her mother died from alcoholism and her older sister was killed in a drive-by shooting, Patrice went to live with relatives. She started drinking, smoking marijuana, and later using cocaine; her relatives began to accuse her of being "just like your mother."

The tribe located a foster family for Patrice to live with; however, her alcohol and other drug use increased, and she began having suicidal ideation frequently. When she overdosed twice, she was sent to the residential treatment center.

Patrice felt responsible for the deaths of her mother and older sister, although the facts clearly showed that this was not true. She felt guilty over not having been able to "save" them. After Patrice did Activity #17 and answered the processing questions, the following dialogue ensued in group:

Patrice I tried to get my stepfather to stop; I used to cry and scream and beg my mother to help me, but she was drunk. . . . She ignored me. . . .

Peer What was he doing to you?

P He locked me in a room, in the dark. . . . He gave me a bucket for a bathroom.

Peer Where were your sisters?

P My little sister tried to help me; she would sneak food under the door, and she hit my stepfather to try to get him to stop hurting us.

Therapist Us?

P Yeah, he used to beat my mother and my sisters too. I guess that's why my mother didn't help me. She was too scared of him. . . . I never told anybody this, but I'm afraid I'm going to get in an abusive relationship just like my mother. I've already been slapped around by guys. . . .

T How will you be able to tell that it's an abusive relationship?

P Because he'll hit me.

Peer You can tell way before that!

P How?

T Let's go back over what you experienced when we did the activity. . . .

As the group continued, Patrice related that she had experienced a "funny" feeling as her partner walked toward her. She had wanted to say "Stop!" before she actually did, but she had not wanted to hurt her partner's feelings by saying "Stop!" Peers gave Patrice feedback on how her concern for the partner's feelings could put her in danger in a real-life situation. Patrice began to see that she needed to trust her "funny" feeling as a warning or cue that her boundaries were being violated.

Clinical Impressions: Patrice had not been protected by her mother from her stepfather's physical abuse. She felt guilty about being angry at her, especially as she saw her mother as also being a victim of her stepfather. Her older sister had tried to help her, but her death had left Patrice feeling alone in the world, and angry about that as well.

Her repeated trauma of being locked away in the dark for no discernible reason had convinced her that somehow she was "bad" and deserving of this punishment, although she also knew that the stepfather's behavior was wrong. The fact that she had already been in physically abusive relationships with teenage boys scared Patrice because she experienced herself as helpless to stop the abuse. She was also scared because she thought she could not read the warning signals as to who was an abuser and who was not. Participating in this activity enabled her to begin expressing her fears for the first time, make connections to the past, and learn new skills about setting boundaries.

❏ **Activity #18: My Personal Space**

Objective: To reinforce the notion of a healthy sense of "personal space."

This activity is designed to reinforce the notion of a personal space around the individual. It is important for adolescents to develop an understanding and a sense of what constitutes healthy personal space. Teens need to find a balance such that they are not too rigid but do not allow others to disrespect their boundaries.

This is a difficult concept for adolescents abused as children because developmentally they may not understand the limits of healthy and unhealthy interactions with others. The adolescent abused as a child may have been in the position of having to set and maintain appropriate and safe boundaries. This responsibility placed the child in a vulnerable position. Therefore, the teen's perceived notion of healthy boundaries or personal space may be skewed.

This activity is designed to help the adolescent explore how he or she envisions personal space.

Ages: This activity is designed for adolescents from 13 years through 18 years.

Materials Needed: Activity sheet and pencils, crayons, markers, and/or colored pencils.

Instructions: Instruct the teen to draw a picture of him- or herself and then to color in the area that he or she designates as his or her personal space. It should be pointed out that this area is the space needed to feel generally safe. It is interesting to note how much personal space is needed around the body.

Note: This activity can serve as another yardstick of the teen's comfort level. For example, a very small "personal space" may indicate an inability to protect oneself. An unreasonably large area may indicate a person who feels vulnerable and therefore needs greater protection. Either way, the following process questions may help in your assessment.

Processing: After this activity is completed, it is important to process the teen's feelings regarding personal space. We have found it helpful to follow up with queries such as "Tell me about your personal space on your picture" and "Is your personal space the same with everyone you know, or do you have a different space for different people? Why or why not?"

□ **Activity #19: Sean's Story**

Objective: To explore the definitions of appropriate and inappropriate social behaviors as they relate to the story presented.

This activity is designed to explore the definitions of appropriate and inappropriate social behaviors. The concept of personal and private space will be discussed. Abused adolescents are often unaware or confused regarding the concept of appropriate social behaviors due to their abusive histories. They may not protect their own boundaries as a result of not appreciating their right to have personal space.

Storytelling can be a nonthreatening way of exploring and learning healthy concepts. However, stories may elicit underlying thoughts and feelings associated with prior abuse histories. Thus, while you are reading this story, it is important to be aware of both verbal and nonverbal responses that the teen may express.

Ages: This activity is appropriate for adolescents from 13 years through 18 years of age.

Materials Needed: Activity sheet and pencil, crayons, markers, and/ or colored pencils.

Instructions: Instruct the individual (or group) to read the story and answer the questions at the end of the story.

Processing: After the story has been read, it is important to process feelings related to the story and other feelings that may have been elicited by the story.

The following case example will illustrate how one sexually and emotionally abused adolescent processed this activity.

Case Example: *Raphael*

Brief Case History: Raphael was a 15-year-old Mexican American teenager who lived at home with his biological parents and an older brother, Jose, age 26. He had been admitted to the acute unit of a psychiatric hospital after two unsuccessful suicide attempts. Raphael told his doctor that he had wanted to die because he had been raped at knifepoint by an unknown older teenage boy. He said he had been too embarrassed to tell his parents. His doctor reported the alleged rape to the police, who sent a detective to interview Raphael. Raphael could give the detective very little information, and the case was dropped. Because Raphael was still depressed, he was referred to intensive outpatient individual and group work for trauma recovery.

For the first three sessions, Raphael spent his time in group complaining about vague physical problems or saying that he never got time to talk. The group leaders were becoming concerned about his lack of participation and his passivity. In one session, the group was asked to read "Sean's Story" and then answer the questions for further discussion. The following dialogue ensued.

Therapist Raphael, can you tell us how you think Sean's boundaries were violated?

Raphael Well, I'm not really sure. . . . Does it have anything to do with how the sister would just walk in his room? That doesn't seem right. . . . I know that would make me mad. My brother used to do that to me. . . .

T Yes, the sister in the story and in your life, Raphael, your brother walking in your room, that is an example of having your boundaries violated. Was your door closed?

R Yeah, he would just walk in without knocking, like in the story.

Peer So what did you do? I would just beat the crap out of him!

R I couldn't do that. I love my brother. . . . Besides, he's 26 years old. He's like a dad to me. I can't tell him what to do.

Peer You could tell your parents. Maybe they could tell him not to do it anymore.

R I thought of that, but my father isn't around much, and when he is, he's usually drunk. I don't want to talk to him. And my mother thinks that my brother is the most wonderful person in the world. He's her favorite (gives a big sigh).

T It doesn't really seem fair, does it?

R No, sometimes it makes me really mad!
T So, what are you going to do about this?
R I don't think there's anything I can do.

The group went on to discuss personal and private space and then drew a picture of Sean.

Clinical Impressions: Raphael felt he did not have a right to privacy in his own bedroom, although he knew it made him uncomfortable when his brother would just walk in. He looked up to his brother as a father and did not want to jeopardize this special relationship in any way. He knew how much his mother depended on her eldest son for emotional and financial support, and he felt cautious about saying anything to her that might make it look as if he was being critical. In short, Raphael was walking "on eggs" in his own home, afraid to say anything about his needs for fear of upsetting a fragile situation. No one had ever confronted his father's alcoholism or the fact that the 26-year-old brother still lived at home.

In another session, Raphael was urged by his peers to role-play telling his brother to please knock before he came into his bedroom. During the role play, Raphael's anger at the entire family situation began to emerge. He was especially mad that he had not been able to tell anyone about the rape; it turned out that his suicide attempts had been faked so that the family would take him seriously. Although Raphael still felt very depressed, he told his peers that he felt better now that this was off his chest. Raphael was resistant to encouragement from the group leaders and his peers to bring this to family therapy with his mother and brother. Consultation with the family therapist alerted her to the situation so that she could help Raphael take the initiative.

❏ **Activity #20: Identifying Healthy and Unhealthy Boundaries**

Objective: To aid the teen in identifying and exploring the extent to which he or she has healthy or unhealthy boundaries. As this is a writing exercise, the teen will have time to think through his or her feelings and thoughts. Hopefully, this will generate increased awareness of how perhaps the teen has displayed poor boundaries and in what areas his or her boundaries are clear and strong.

Ages: This activity is appropriate for more mature teens who are capable of formal operational thinking. It requires the ability to think abstractly and conceptualize a full range of boundaries.

Materials Needed: Activity sheet and pen or pencil.

Instructions: Instruct the teen or group to read the list in the *Activity Book.* Teens are to choose one example they think is a healthy boundary, one that is unhealthy, and one that is perhaps questionable. After noting on the sheet which is which, ask them to write about a time they experienced one of the above in their lives. This can be done as homework or during the session. If it is done in session, ask the teen to confine him- or herself to approximately 15 minutes of writing time.

Processing: After the writing is completed, engage the individual/ group in sharing definitions and experiences. In a group setting, peers can offer the participant feedback as to whether they agree with the participant's definitions of healthy, unhealthy, and questionable boundaries. An important prelude to the discussion is to acknowledge that what is questionable for one teen may be clearly defined for another. Individual morals and values as well as "safety" concerns (e.g., a potentially abusive situation) will most likely be raised during the discussion, which may become rather heated.

❑ **Activity #21: Boundaries and Personal Space**

Objective: To assess the teen's understanding of boundaries and personal space.

By the time the activities in this chapter are completed, the teen should have a working definition of *boundaries* and *personal space.* This activity is designed to elicit each individual's own understanding of how he or she experiences the meaning of *boundaries* and *personal space*. The essay part of this activity is purposefully left open-ended so as not to influence the teen's perceptions.

Ages: This activity is designed for adolescents of all ages. The level of each teen's development will dictate the quality of the response.

Materials Needed: Activity sheet and pencil or pen.

Instructions: Instruct the teen to complete the activity sheet in their *Activity Book.* Some teens will give a cursory definition and concrete statement reiterating what has previously been discussed. It is important to encourage them to come up with their own definition and experience. It is best to give this as a homework assignment so as not to limit their expression.

Note: The educationally challenged or learning-disabled teen may need to dictate the responses to you.

Processing: After the teen is finished writing, encourage an open discussion. In a group setting, this can be accomplished by first having different teens read their responses. In individual therapy, the teen can read his or her response to you, and a discussion can ensue about boundaries and personal space. This gives you an opportunity to assess the progress in recovery to this point. You may need to make a decision as to whether further work is needed in this area before progressing to Chapter 5, "Developing Trust and Being Safe."

PHASE II

Exploration of Trauma

5

Developing Trust and Being Safe

Children are born with an instinct to trust and a basic innocence that make them easy targets for abuse. When this trust is violated, the innocence of childhood is lost. Abuse shatters children's trust and violates their basic instincts and perceptions of others, leaving them emotionally vulnerable and targeting them for revictimization. They no longer feel "safe." If the abuser was the parent or another trusted adult figure, the sense of betrayal is even greater (Bolton & Bolton, 1987; Finkelhor & Browne, 1986; Herman, 1981; Malchiodi, 1990; Sgroi, 1982).

Many abused adolescents experienced the abuse in earlier stages of development. Therefore, many statements attributed to "child victims" are also relevant to the adolescent victim. Periodically, we make reference to "child" victims in this book. We are attempting to convey the damage that occurred earlier in the adolescents' development and has significant impact on their current functioning.

Finkelhor and Browne (1986) proposed a model that can be used to understand the initial and long-term effects of child sexual abuse.

The model includes four trauma-causing factors that they referred to as *traumagenic dynamics*—traumatic sexualization, stigmatization, betrayal, and powerlessness.

The term *betrayal dynamic* refers to the sense of a betrayal of trust experienced by the child sexual abuse victim. Although Finkelhor and Browne attributed this dynamic to child sexual abuse, we have found that this sense of betrayal can also be found with victims of physical and emotional abuse or neglect.

Webb (1991) described the betrayal dynamic in children as leading to difficulties in interpersonal relationships, including guardedness, suspiciousness, ambivalence, and choice of relationships in which one is exploited. In addition, antisocial attitudes and behaviors may evolve in response to the rage and anger associated with the sense of betrayal.

In addition to the betrayal dynamic, abused children are often stigmatized by negative statements made by the abuser. These children are often made to feel as if they are the ones who are "crazy," and many times they are made to feel responsible for the inappropriate and abusive actions of others. It is not unusual for perpetrators to tell their victims such things as "You made me do it," "If you weren't so sexy . . . ," "You made me angry," "You're stupid," or "You're just like your father/mother."

The child's reality is often negated by such statements as "That's not true," "He or she wouldn't have done that," "You're lying," or "You're just making it up." The internalization, during or following child abuse, of these negative statements and judgments made by others frequently produces guilt, shame, and self-blame (Briere, 1992; Courtois, 1988). Finkelhor and Browne (1986) referred to this as the *stigmatization dynamic.*

Webb (1991) listed self-deprecating behaviors, self-mutilating behaviors, and self-destructive behaviors as common manifestations of the stigmatization dynamic. The result is abuse-related poor self-esteem (Briere, 1992).

Another phenomenon that you may note in your work with traumatized adolescents is the *traumatic bond.* Traumatic bonding, as defined by Dutton and Painter (1981), is "the strong emotional tie between two persons where one person intermittently harasses, beats, threatens, abuses or intimidates the other" (pp. 146-147). According to Ewing (1987), this phenomenon has been observed between hostages and their captors, battered children and their abusive parents, cult members and their oppressive leaders, and concentration camp prisoners and their guards.

Two common features of traumatic bonding are an imbalance of power and the intermittence of the abuse, alternating with a return to more normal and "acceptable" interactions. Adolescents in this situation find themselves conflicted and torn as they engage in therapy. They often become overwhelmed when they get in touch with the painful aspects of the abusive relationship due to the unhealthy allegiance that is formed by the intermittent nature of the abuse.

Adolescents or children who have had their trust and safety violated react to their environments in diverse ways. Some become hypervigilant, reacting to even the mildest stimulus. Others become apathetic, appearing not to care who or what invades their environment. Still others perceive any form of maltreatment as associated with danger, or even, in some cases, fear of impending death (Conte, Briere, & Sexton, 1989). Therefore, the abused individual must first learn what healthy trust is. This process begins with learning to trust oneself.

The goal of this chapter is to help the adolescent understand trust and learn how to be "safe." Helping the teen establish trust and learning the dynamics of a safe relationship is an essential objective in trauma resolution work. The activities in this chapter are designed to assist in the process of attaining this goal.

Since the focus in this chapter is on trust and safety, the teen may begin testing the limits of the relationship with you as his or her therapist. This testing is to ensure that you will be a safe person who maintains a healthy balance between unconditional acceptance and limit setting. Therefore, maintaining this balance will be critical throughout your work.

We have included a few case studies and examples of actual dialogue to help you in further understanding how some of these activities have been used in therapy sessions. As we have previously stated, it is important to engage in thorough processing of each activity. Therefore, we have included a section called "Processing" to assist you in your discussions. These questions are general, so you may want to adapt questions to suit the adolescent's individual needs.

As with the other chapters, the *Activity Book* includes a "Teen Talk" section that introduces the topic of the chapter in more teenage-appropriate language. You will want to read this section as well as having the teen read the section in his or her book before doing the activities.

❏ Activity #22: Sara's Story

Objective: To explore the concept of feeling safe by reading about one girl's story.

This activity is designed to explore the concept of feeling safe. The story presented in this activity portrays a 10-year-old girl put in charge of her 2-year-old brother. The teen is challenged to evaluate the appropriateness of the mother's decision regarding having her daughter left in charge of her little brother, as well as other questionable decisions.

Although this story was designed to be a simple introduction to the concept of safety, it may elicit a significant amount of discomfort, depending on the teen's childhood experiences. Aiding the teen in identifying the source of discomfort may encourage him or her to share more openly. Because the child in the story is so much younger, it may provide enough distance for the teen to make a more "objective" evaluation of a potentially dangerous situation.

Ages: This activity is appropriate for teens 13 through 18 years of age. Even learning-disabled teens should have little difficulty reading this story.

Materials Needed: Activity Book and pencils, crayons, markers, and/ or colored pencils.

Instructions: Instruct the teen to read the story and complete the questions. Process the questions after they are completed. This makes for an interesting discussion.

Processing: After the teen is finished reading the story, we have found it helpful to discuss the story by going over the questions in the *Activity Book* or follow up with questions such as "What do you think about the story?" "Tell me what *being safe* means to you," "Have there ever been times when you didn't feel safe? Why or why not?" and "Tell me about your picture."

Case Example: *Chris*

Brief Case History: Chris was a 14-year-old Caucasian male who identified as gay and a cross-dresser. He described himself as "always" having known that he was attracted to men and not to women. Chris had been found prostituting himself on the street after having run away from his second foster home. Chris was under the care of Child Protective Services (CPS) since he had been removed from his mother's home 2 years earlier. His mother, an active alcoholic, had been physically and emotionally abusive to Chris. She had kept him home from school to take care of her.

At age 8, Chris had learned how to prepare his mother's and her friends' favorite drinks. He did the laundry and cooked while his mother was drunk or in a stupor. A neighbor had called CPS several times to check on Chris. When he was suspected of molesting a 6-year-old boy (no charges were ever pressed), CPS removed him from the home. After running away from the foster homes (no younger children were in the home), Chris was placed in a residential treatment facility.

In a group therapy session, Chris and his peers were asked to complete the above activity. The following dialogue ensued.

Therapist Chris, what did you think of the story?

Chris Well, most people said that Sara was too young to watch her brother, but I disagree. She was old enough. . . . I did a lot of things when I was 8!

T Do you think Sara felt safe?

C No. . . . She was scared . . . but nothing really bad happened to her, did it? She just kept her door closed and she was okay.

Peer What about the part when she saw her mother getting hit?

C You think that's a big deal? Worse things happen than that!

T   Do you think you would feel safe in that situation?

C   Yeah. . . . I would do what she did—just keep my door shut, maybe turn on some music so I couldn't hear the yelling. . . .

T   Sounds like you have some experience with this kind of situation.

C   Oh, my mother used to get so drunk, she'd be falling down and I'd have to help her to bed. And she would bring these guys home. . . . But I don't really want to talk about that in here. They (referring to his peers) already call me so many names, I don't want them to say bad things about my mother.

T   That's okay, you don't have to talk about it right now, although perhaps you'd be willing to talk to your individual therapist about it.

C   Maybe. . . .

T   So, Chris, what does being "safe" mean to you?

C   I really don't know. . . . Do you mean like not getting beat up or molested?

T   That could be part of being safe, definitely, but what does a person need, in a positive way, to be safe?

C   I have no idea what you mean.

Peer Can I help him out?

The group session continued while the group members brainstormed about what being safe meant to them. The therapist wrote all of their ideas on the board, and the ideas were discussed.

Clinical Impressions: Chris was obviously a bright young man. Although he completely identified with his caretaker role in the family, he was willing to actively talk about the concepts of "safe" and "not safe" in an effort to understand. Chris was quite realistic about the negative attitudes his peers held about homosexuality and was only willing to expose so much about his background. What he did not share in this session was that one of his mother's boyfriends had molested him over a period of a year when he was 7 years old. Chris could easily tell you this was "wrong," but he seemed completely detached from any affect whatsoever. His life experiences were an interesting "story" to him.

In his individual work, Chris shared that he actually felt safest on the street hustling because he felt wanted there. Further exploration revealed that Chris's only sources of self-esteem were his desirability as a sex object and his role as his mother's caretaker. He could not afford to challenge his mother's demands of him because he saw her as the only person in the world that he had any ties to. In individual sessions, Chris also revealed his penchant for cross-dressing.

Being in the group for a long period of time eventually broke down some of Chris's defenses. His peers accepted him, even though sometimes they still made rude jokes about his sexuality. This was Chris's first experience in a group with age-mates talking about his emotional needs as an abused adolescent. He really had no idea there was any other way to live beyond what he had experienced at home. Listening to his peers and seeing that they actually wanted to help him was a therapeutic eye-opener for Chris. Chris began to identify group as a safe place for him.

Briere (1992) referred to some victims as suffering from "other-directedness," meaning that they dependent on understanding the demands of others. They become hypervigilant and are always anticipating what others expect of them. This seemed to be the case with Chris. He was tuned into what was going on with others rather than focusing on his own needs. This activity highlighted Chris's ongoing therapeutic needs, which included developing healthier boundaries, experiencing his feelings associated with his traumatic past, and learning to trust himself so that he would be better able to take care of his own needs.

With regard to the cross-dressing, Chris's grandmother used to dress him in girls' clothing when he was very young. He continued this activity because of the gratification he received from it. It was unclear whether this was a gender/identity issue or part of his past learned behavior. Identity confusion is part of the diagnosis of Borderline Personality Disorder, commonly found in adults abused as children. Therefore, this could be an indication of an emerging personality disorder. The cross-dressing had nothing to do with his sexual orientation. It had to do with finding an acceptable identity. Chris was determined to continue this behavior in addition to the prostitution. He loved exotic dancing and had no desire to give this up. All attempts to challenge him on his decisions were met with resistance. Individual and group therapy continued to address these important issues.

❑ **Activity #23: My Safest Place**

Objective: To determine where the teen feels safest in his or her environment.

This activity is designed to determine where the adolescent feels safest in his or her environment. Although a teen may identify several places where he or she feels safe, it is important to single out the one place that feels the safest so as to determine whether the place given is truly a safe place. For example, if the teen names his or her "homies'" house as the safest place and it is notorious for drive-by shootings, a discussion of the reality of this situation needs to be addressed.

In addition, having the teen identify the place where he or she feels the safest can assist in the therapeutic process. By simply sharing this place with you, the teen is acknowledging a sense of trust on some level. Also, you will be able to reference this place as you proceed through the process of healing.

Ages: This activity is designed for adolescents of all ages.

Materials Needed: Activity sheet and pencils, crayons, markers, and/ or colored pencils.

Instructions: Instruct the teen to think about all the places where he or she feels safe. Then have the teen choose the place where he or she feels the safest. After one place has been identified, instruct him or her to write an essay about this place. A drawing may be added if desired.

Processing: After the activity is completed, have the teen read the essay to you or to the group. Additional questions may be asked, such as "What makes this place safe to you?" and "What makes this place safer to you than other places?"

❑ **Activity #24: Unsafe Places**

Objective: To identify and discuss the places where the teen feels unsafe.

This activity is designed to encourage the teen to identify and explore the places where he or she feels unsafe. Just as it is important to identify places that feel safe, it is equally important to help identify places that feel unsafe. It is important for abused teens to clarify their safe and unsafe places early in treatment. If they become confused about safe or unsafe places later in treatment, you can remind them of what they previously stated. This gives them the opportunity to reassess what they said earlier in the therapeutic process and determine which perception is more reality based.

Ages: This activity is designed for ages 13 through 18 years.

Materials Needed: Activity sheet (extra paper may be needed) and pencils, crayons, markers, and/or colored pencils.

Instructions: Instruct the teen to think about various places where he or she feels unsafe. Then instruct the teen to write an essay about one or more of those places. If the teen refuses or states that there is no place where he or she feels unsafe, encourage him or her to write about the place that is the least comfortable to him or her.

Processing: After the activity is completed, it is helpful to process the activity by having the teen read the essay. Additional questions are "What makes these places unsafe for you? Why?" "How did you feel while you were writing about your unsafe place(s)?" and "Which place felt the most unsafe?"

❑ **Activity #25: Brian's Story**

Objective: To process the concept of trust through storytelling.

This activity is designed to explore the teen's concept of trust. This story is about a young teen's struggle with an abusive older brother. It may elicit strong reactions. Sibling abuse is a serious problem that is often ignored and minimized by the abused teen. We have found many teens who identified with this story. It stimulates lots of discussion.

Ages: This activity is appropriate for adolescents of all ages.

Materials Needed: Activity sheets and pencils, crayons, markers, and/or colored pencils.

Instructions: Instruct the teen to read "Brian's Story" in the activity book. After the teen has read it, instruct him or her to complete the questions and draw the picture.

Processing: After reading the story, process the given questions. We have found it helpful to ask additional questions such as "What do you think about the story?" "Have there ever been people whom you felt you could not trust? Why/why not?" and "Tell me about your picture."

❑ **Activity #26: People I Trust**

Objective: To continue processing and learning about the concept of trust.

This activity is designed to explore further the concept of trust. It is hoped that teens will be able to relate the abstract concept of trust to both peers and adults in their life.

The word *trust* is such a common word used in our society that teens might lose the concept of what underlies this word. Although the media has tended to overuse this word in the past, today many people tend to "distrust" more than "trust" people. Therefore, it is not surprising that teens have picked up a cynical notion of trust.

Adolescents who have been abused as children have often been abused by the person they are supposed to trust. Often, the abuser has been left in charge of the child or has assumed some kind of power over the child. These children have become confused adolescents due to the contradiction between what they have been told about trust and what they have actually experienced.

Ages: Adolescents of all ages should have very few problems with this activity.

Materials Needed: Activity sheet and pencils.

Instructions: Instruct the teen to think about the person(s) whom he or she trusts. Then tell him or her to list and explain why the person(s) are trustworthy.

Processing: After the teen completes the list, it is important to process the answers by asking questions such as "What makes you think you can trust this person?" and "How do you feel about this person? Why?" Group feedback is encouraged when processing this in a group setting.

Case Example: *Annie*

Brief Case History: Annie was a 16-year-old female Caucasian who had run away from home 3 years before. Since then, she had been placed in a variety of settings such as foster and group homes and shelters; she had run away 15 times. She was arrested for some of these runaways. She had also stolen a gun from her sister's home.

For the past year, Annie had been living with a 30-year-old man named Tom. According to Annie, this man controlled her movements, severely beat her, and pistol-whipped and kicked her. Sometimes they would have consensual sex; other times "he made me." Annie was using crystal methamphetamine on a daily basis with Tom. After they broke into Annie's sister's home to steal money, the police were contacted. Tom was arrested, and Annie was brought to the acute unit of a psychiatric hospital.

According to Annie, Tom would not let her call her mother, so she felt she was being "held captive"; she would slash her wrists in an effort to get him to let her go home. She reported nightmares and flashbacks and showed an increased startle response and hypervigilance during her hospital stay. During an evaluation for trauma symptoms, Annie told the interviewer that she "loved" Tom. Her affect seemed unnaturally bright when she listed the serious injuries he had inflicted on her. Annie frequently defended Tom, telling staff that they did not really "understand" him and that she hoped that he would not have to go to jail.

According to the 27-year-old sister, the family had always thought there was a possibility that Annie's 29-year-old brother (now living in another state) had molested Annie when she was around 5 years old. This was never confirmed, nor did Annie receive any counseling at the time. Annie was viewed as a "liar and sneak" in the family and had never done well academically despite her high IQ.

After it was ascertained that Annie was not a danger to herself, she was transferred to a residential treatment program. There, she continued to maintain the Tom was "really a good guy—we had good times together." She seemed unwilling or perhaps unable to talk about him negatively for more than perhaps two sentences. Although her peers continually gave her feedback about the abusive nature of their relationship, Annie would just say, "I know" and shrug. She claimed to miss him, and one day when she was very angry at a peer, she stated she would rather be with Tom than in the residential treatment center.

Therapist What is it about being with Tom that would help you now?

Annie I don't know—but I felt safe with him.

T Did you trust him?

A Well, I don't really know what that means. . . . (Annie had her hands clasped over her chest.) It's funny, my chest feels all tight, like I can't breathe. . . .

T Let's see if we can help you relax. I'll give you your favorite stuffed animal to hold. . . . Now take a deep breath and look around you. . . . Where are you? Can you describe the room?

A Yeah. . . . This is your office. The rug is blue, and you have lots of animals and books. (She took another breath.) I feel better now.

T Okay—did you notice that even though you said you felt safe with Tom, as soon as we started talking about that you felt like you couldn't breathe?

A Yeah. . . . I don't want to talk about it anymore.

T That's fine. . . . I would like you to write in your journal this week and make note of any time during the day or night that you get that funny feeling in your chest or if you can't breathe.

A Do I have to?

T No, you don't have to. Let's just have you write about whatever you want to.

Clinical Impressions: It definitely appeared that Annie was suffering from having established a traumatic bond with Tom. Annie had become so cognitively dissociated from her fear of him that the only ways she experienced it were somatically and during nightmares. For her to let down her defenses enough to examine her lack of trust in this person would be to overwhelm her conscious being with terror. Therefore, she tried to stay focused on the "good" Tom, the one who seemed strong and who wanted her so much that he would even resort to hurting her to make her stay. Although this reasoning may seem difficult to comprehend, for the victim traumatically bonded with his or her abuser it makes perfect sense. Unfortunately, unless Annie could feel safe enough in her treatment setting to develop trust, she might find herself revictimized.

The possibility that Annie's trust was betrayed at age 5 by her brother, the lack of involvement by her mother, and any organic damage created by her drug abuse all complicated her treatment. This was an adolescent girl who required long-term treatment with consistent caregivers. If discharged prematurely, Annie might well run away again.

❏ **Activity #27: Broken Trust**

Objective: To identify ways that trust can be broken.

This activity is designed to allow the teen to identify ways that trust can be broken. This activity may elicit powerful feelings because the teen will be associating specific acts perpetrated on him or her while writing the essay.

Although this activity is designed to elicit specific ways that trust can be violated, some teens may write in a more superficial way. If the teen is more serious about this activity, he or she may experience inner turmoil. Therefore, you may observe behaviors that reflect this turmoil. Be aware of this and be prepared!

This activity may be difficult for some teens because it may be the first time the "code of silence" has been threatened to be broken. It is difficult to anticipate just what the teen has been told by the perpetrator to keep him or her "silent." It is important not to make judgments about what is told to you, especially if the teen tells you that he or she enjoyed the experience. This needs to be explored with the teen so that he or she may come to his or her own conclusions.

Another critical aspect of the teen's revealing of the abuser is the therapist's duty to report. The person identified by the teen is a possible abuser and must be reported to the proper authorities. You should familiarize yourself with the child abuse reporting laws in your state.

Ages: This activity is designed for adolescents of all ages. The more mature teen will most likely include more detail.

Materials Needed: Activity sheet and pencils or pen.

Instructions: Instruct the teen to write an essay about a time when someone broke his or her trust. The teen can also include other people that he or she has trouble trusting.

Processing: After completing this activity, have the teen read his or her essay to you or the group. Additional questions may be asked, such as "Have other people broken your trust in them? How?" "How does it feel to have your trust broken? Why?" "How are you taking care of yourself now?" and "What have you learned about trust?"

❏ Activity #28: Being Assertive!

Objective: To assist teens in developing assertiveness skills.

This activity is designed to assist teens in developing assertiveness skills to help protect them against future abuses. Abused teens often find themselves in "victim" roles, being either passive or passive-aggressive. They may have difficulty differentiating between what is assertive and what is aggressive. Activity #17 (Stop!) was the first step toward a better understanding of assertiveness.

To introduce the activity, first help the individual teen or the group you are working with to define what assertiveness, passivity, and aggressiveness mean to them. The following definitions were adapted from *Pattern Changing for Abused Women* (Goodman & Fallon, 1995, Suppl.) and may aid in clarifying these terms.

- *Assertiveness:* Expressing oneself—one's needs, wants or feelings—without violating the rights of others; being honest, sincere, and direct.
- *Passivity:* Not expressing oneself; allowing others to take advantage of you. Not saying what or how you feel. Avoiding conflict and confrontation.
- *Aggressiveness:* Expressing your feelings, wants, and needs at the expense of others. Violating others, dominating them. Using physical or verbal intimidation to get your way.

The following activity has two steps. First, the teen will identify which vignettes typify passivity, assertiveness, or aggressiveness and will rewrite the passive and aggressive responses as assertive responses. Next, the teen will role-play with you in individual therapy or with peers in group therapy.

Ages: This activity is designed for teens of all ages. However, the less mature teen may have some difficulty with these concepts.

Materials Needed: Activity sheet and pencil or pen.

Instructions and Processing:

Step 1: Instruct the teen to read each vignette in the activity book, determining whether it represents an assertive, passive, or aggressive response to the problem and to rewrite the response, if necessary, in the blank provided. Next, process the responses. You may want to ask questions such as "Do you think this was an appropriate response?" and "How could you change this response to be assertive?" If working in a group you may want to ask, "Does everyone agree?" and, if not, "How can we change this so everyone agrees?" Once the processing is finished, go to Step 2.

Step 2: Once consensus on assertive responses has been reached, instruct the teen or group to engage in role-playing each vignette. If working in individual therapy, you will need to participate in the role play.

After each vignette has been role-played, the teen(s) should engage in processing. During processing, you will want to include questions such as "How did you feel in your role?" "Was it comfortable being assertive/having someone else being assertive with you?" and "Do you think you could use these skills in daily life situations?"

❑ Activity #29: Safety Rules

Objective: To develop rules that will assist in safeguarding the teen against experiencing any future abuse.

This activity is designed to assist the teen in developing a set of rules that will assist him or her in safeguarding against experiencing any future abuse. Developing a set of rules to keep safe and to keep others safe, as well as internalizing these rules, is imperative to the abused teen's healing process. Therefore, this process will need to be repeated and reviewed as the teen progresses through the *Activity Book.*

Ages: This activity is designed for adolescents of all ages.

Materials Needed: Activity sheet and pencils or pens.

Instructions: Instruct the teen to read the listed rules. Then instruct him or her to list five additional ways to keep him- or herself safe. Encourage an open discussion of ways to keep safe. Refrain from giving your ideas so as not to discourage the teen from coming up with his or her own ideas of what constitutes rules to keep safe.

Processing: After the teen completes the list, it is important to discuss the rules. We have found it helpful to follow up with questions such as "How do you feel about the rules listed?" "Which rule do you feel is the safest? Why?" "Tell me about your rules," and "How will these rules keep you safe?"

6

Secrets

It is often said that we are only as sick as our secrets. For most abused children and adolescents, silence becomes a survival mechanism. Maintaining this silence adds to the underlying feelings of guilt and shame, thereby increasing the likelihood that the abuse will continue unnoticed, unreported, or undisclosed.

Once trust is established between you and the adolescent, it is necessary to begin uncovering the hidden secrets. This is a very difficult and frightening process for most abused adolescents because the pressure to keep the secret is experienced psychologically as fear (Burgess & Holmstrom, 1978). As children, many adolescents were threatened or coerced to maintain silence. Often they were threatened with abandonment or rejection with comments such as "If you tell, I'll kill you," "If you tell, mommy and daddy will get divorced," "If you tell, your parents won't love you," or "If you tell, you'll get in trouble." As adolescents, these threats may become even more graphic or intense. Others have difficulty breaking the silence for fear that they will not be believed or will be blamed for the abuse.

Burgess and Holmstrom (1978) referred to the dominant-subordinate role as another reason that children remain silent. Children are in the subordinate role in most situations, with the exception of peer-related interactions. Therefore, they often view authority figures as setting the standard of what is right and wrong (i.e., if adults do it, it must be right).

A problem unique to young children is the communication barrier that naturally exists. The child often has difficulty verbalizing his or her experiences in adult language. It is highly unlikely that a young child will go up to an adult and explain in meaningful language exactly what happened. For one thing, if the abuser has approached the child in a nonthreatening manner, the child may not realize the behavior was "wrong." Adolescents you are working with may have experienced the above scenario and may now be disclosing their abuse for the first time.

Gil (1991) pointed out that even when children are spared overt threats, many of them seem to sense the secrecy of family violence or sexual abuse. They may feel that they should not talk about family matters. This is often conditioned over time. The same is true for adolescents.

Abused adolescents typically need to know the difference between *secrecy* and *privacy*. It is important for them to understand the need for privacy, which can be empowering. However, adolescents required to keep secrets for years feel burdened by this task and are left with an overwhelming sense of helplessness.

The terms *secrecy* and *privacy* are often confused. In fact, it is not uncommon for abused children and teens to say that they cannot talk about something that happened to them because it is "private." They need to sort out the difference between feeling empowered to share the secret that has kept them alienated from others and the right to privacy, such as spending time in their room alone or to listen to their personal stereo or Walkman.

Abused adolescents need a warm, nurturing, and safe environment in order to share their painful secrets. Talking about the abuse history is vital in the recovery process. However, these adolescents need to understand that it is not necessary to share their secrets with everyone. Because abused children and teens typically have a problem with appropriate boundaries, they sometimes indiscriminately share information. This may leave them vulnerable to revictimization, blame by others who do not fully understand child abuse and its effects, or criticism from their peers.

The goal of this chapter is to assist teens in revealing their secrets and breaking their silence. The activities in this chapter are designed to assist in identifying, disclosing, and processing "secrets." Although reactions to disclosure vary considerably, a recent study by Berliner and Conte (1995) suggested that most children felt that disclosing their victimization was a "good" thing. However, this can also be a very painful process for the abused adolescent.

During this period of time, you may observe the "acting out" of conflicts in the form of regressive or aggressive behaviors. This can be quite disconcerting to the therapist or other people involved with the adolescent's treatment. It is important to support the teen as he or she begins to process the "secrets" that have been locked up for so long. In addition to the activities outlined in this chapter, play therapy has been found to be an excellent therapeutic tool in processing traumatic events with younger or more regressed teens (Gil, 1991; Webb, 1991).

A few case studies and specific examples of some of the activities in this chapter are provided to clarify how some of these activities have been used in actual therapy situations. We hope this helps you in your work with abused adolescents.

Before beginning the activities in this chapter, you may want to read the section "Teen Talk" in the *Activity Book* and have the adolescent read this section in his or her book. This will give a brief introduction to the activities below.

❏ **Activity #30: Nikki's Story**

Objective: To begin discussing the concept of secrets through storytelling.

This activity is designed to explore the difference between "safe" secrets and "unsafe" secrets. It is normal for adolescents to share secrets with their friends. However, for the abused teen, secrets pose a confusing dilemma.

Although this story was designed to explore one teenage girl's dilemma as she struggled with conflicting loyalties, it may trigger memories or feelings of the teen's own abuse history. You, as the therapist, need to be acutely aware of body language, statements made, and behavioral changes. These may be "red flags" that the teen is struggling with thoughts, feelings, or "secrets" that need to be addressed.

Ages: This activity is appropriate for adolescents of all ages.

Materials Needed: Activity sheet and pencils.

Instructions: Instruct the teen to read "Nikki's Story" in the *Activity Book.* After the teen has read the story, instruct him or her to complete the questions related to the story. Have the teen read his or her responses.

Note: For the severely learning-disabled teen, the story may need to be read aloud.

Processing: After the teen has completed reading and answering the questions, it is important to process the story. Adolescents seem to enjoy discussing various aspects of the story and may interject some of their own history during the discussion. We have found it helpful to follow up with additional questions such as "What do you think about the story?" "Give me an example of a safe and unsafe secret," "How did you feel about Nikki's secret?" and "Have you ever had a secret that you thought you shouldn't tell?"

Case Example: *Jason*

Brief Case History: Jason was a 15-year-old Caucasian male with learning disabilities and borderline intelligence. He had been placed in a residential treatment facility after having been arrested for sexually molesting a 4-year-old girl in his neighborhood. One of the reasons he was placed in this particular facility was that it was not coed. He had a significant history of lying, stealing, and being destructive and physically assaultive. He had run away from home several times and had poor peer relations. Jason was viewed as being attention seeking and angry and as having a very negative self-image. He had many somatic complaints and nightmares and was worried about losing control.

Jason's mother was unenthusiastic about attending family therapy. She missed several appointments without calling first to cancel. When the therapist confronted her on avoiding the sessions with Jason, the mother explained that there was no hope for Jason. He had hit her more than once, just as his father had, and she just wanted to be left alone to care for her daughter.

As Jason began to make some behavioral progress, the mother did agree to come to visit him briefly and was very surprised that he had not hit any of his peers so far. After 2 months with no major incidents, Jason's mother finally agreed to come to a family therapy session.

On Briere's (1996) Trauma Symptom Checklist for Children (TSCC), Jason had significantly high scores on the Anger and Dissociation subscales. Given Jason's history of property damage, his physical assaultiveness, and the fact that he had already once molested a young child, the treatment team thought it essential that Jason work on his trauma issues in both individual and group therapy.

Due to the fact that Jason was severely learning disabled, the session started with "Nikki's Story" being read to Jason rather than his reading the story to himself. The following processing then took place.

Therapist After listening to the story, Jason, what do you think is the difference between safe and unsafe secrets?

Jason It makes me think about what my father did to my sister. . . . They put him in prison. . . . I should have killed him when I had the chance!

T I know you're very angry that your father hurt your sister—was that a secret in your house?

J Yeah—it turns out that my sister told my mother and she didn't believe her. . . . Then she told me, and I didn't know what to do. My sister said not to tell anyone because then my mother would be even madder at her.

T So, would you call that "safe" or "unsafe"?

J   Well, unsafe, I guess. . . . It wasn't safe to talk about anything in my house! My father used to beat us for nothing when he got drunk!

T   What do you think Nikki's conflict was?

J   She couldn't tell her mother, and she couldn't tell her sisters either about her grandfather molesting her.

T   That's right. What do you think she should do?

J   I think she should call the cops—get him put away. I couldn't tell anybody either. . . .

T   It is hard to tell people about being molested.

J   How did you know? The only person that knows about my father and me is my sister—and I guess my probation officer knows. (Note: This was the first time Jason disclosed that his father had abused him.)

T   What are you on probation for?

J   Well, I touched this little girl, you know, on the leg (points to upper thigh), and then I don't what happened—I just got carried away. I didn't mean any thing bad. . . . She was laughing at first, so I thought it was okay, then she started crying and I thought people would hear her. I was scared, so I let her run home. She told her mother and I got in trouble.

T   Let's see if I understand—you were molested by your father too?

J   Yeah, but I don't want to talk about that. . . . I could kill him for what he did to my sister!

T   Sounds like you still have a secret. You didn't tell CPS that he hurt you too?

J   No way! I'm not a fag or anything! I didn't want my mother to feel even worse.

T   Being molested by a man doesn't make you a "fag," Jason.

J   Well, I know I'm not a fag—look what I did to that little girl. I remember it made me feel all big. . . . I know she liked me.

T   I wonder if there's any connection between your father molesting you and you molesting the girl?

J   That's what people say, but I don't know. . . . As bad as I feel about touching her, I feel worse about what my father did. . . . Please don't make me talk about it in group, please?

T   Of course, I won't make you. It's your decision to tell when you're ready.

Clinical Impressions: This activity was very helpful in getting Jason to open up about his molestation and to process the deep feelings he still had. However, it was obvious that Jason was much more comfortable talking about his sister being molested and his own perpetration on the 4-year-old girl. Jason equated being molested by a male with being a "fag." This would need to be processed further with Jason in later therapy sessions.

It is frightening to note that Jason seemed to get a sense of power and control from his perpetration of abuse on the little girl. Given his past history of physical assaultiveness, his limited cognitive skills, and emotional immaturity, Jason could be at risk for becoming a serious sex offender. Therefore, ongoing intensive therapeutic intervention would be crucial for Jason to become a safe member of society.

❑ Activity #31: It's Confidential!

Objective: To explore what constitutes a safe secret.

This activity is designed to encourage the teen to identify and express "safe" secrets. Adolescents who have been abused often lump all secrets together, assuming that they should not divulge any secrets at all. These teens need to learn how to differentiate between different kinds of secrets as well as learning that it is okay to reveal secrets that are harmful.

A particular problem when dealing with teens is their perceived loyalty to friends or family when faced with disclosing information that could even save another person's life. They tend to want to keep secrets at all costs, especially if they might be perceived as a "narc" or a "snitch."

This activity is designed to assist the teen to differentiate between a truly safe, confidential secret, such as a surprise party or gift, and an unsafe secret. Later activities will address the more difficult secrets.

Ages: This activity is designed for adolescents of all ages.

Materials Needed: Activity sheet and pencils or pens.

Instructions: Instruct the teen to think back to a time when someone told him or her a safe, confidential secret. Then have him or her write an essay about a time when he or she told someone a "confidential" secret.

Processing: After the teen has completed the essay, have him or her read it aloud. We have found it helpful to follow up with queries such as "Tell me about your secret," "Who did you tell your secret to? Why?" "How did you feel when you told your secret?" and "How do you think your friend felt when you told your secret?"

❏ **Activity #32: My Friend's Secret**

Objective: To explore difficult secrets through the medium of writing stories.

This activity is designed to utilize the storytelling technique to encourage the teen to explore his or her difficult secrets. Often teens find it easier to process their own secrets by projecting their experiences onto "a friend's" secret. Asking teens to make up a story about another child allows them to expose their own secrets while pretending that the secrets are someone else's. This frees them up to explore feelings associated with difficult or painful secrets because they do not feel as threatened when attributing feelings to others.

Ages: This activity is designed for adolescents of all ages.

Materials Needed: Activity sheet and pencils.

Instructions: Instruct the teen to think of a story about a kid who has a difficult secret and then to write it on the page provided in the *Activity Book.* Additional pages may be added if needed.

Processing: After the teen is finished writing the story, have him or her read it aloud. It is then important to process. During the processing, we have found it helpful follow up with queries such as "Tell me about your story," "How do you think the person in your story feels about his/her secret?" "Did the kid find someone safe to talk to? Why? Who?" and "Are you like the kid in your story? How?"

❑ Activity #33: Can We Talk?

Objective: To begin exploring who are appropriate and safe people to share secrets with, as well as to begin sharing difficult secrets themselves.

This activity is designed to identify who are appropriate and safe people to share secrets with. It may be necessary to have a discussion of appropriate and safe people before beginning this activity. Younger or more immature teens may be confused by the concept of appropriateness and may not be able to determine which people in their environment are safe.

Many teens abused as children were coerced to keep silent by their abusers. To add to their confusion, the abusers were often people they were "supposed to" trust. Thus, these teens now have difficulty discriminating between people who can be trusted and people who cannot be trusted.

Often times, abused children and teens handle the above dilemma by either refusing to talk at all or talking incessantly to anyone and everyone they come in contact with. Therefore, your discussion with the teen regarding safe and appropriate people to share difficult secrets with is a necessary step in the recovery process.

As well as exploring who to share secrets with, this activity focuses on actual secrets. Therefore, it may bring up unpleasant memories. It is important for you, as the therapist, to be extremely sensitive to the difficulty of this process. It may provoke a variety of feelings that can become somewhat overwhelming. Teens use many defense mechanisms to cope with their abuse histories. Some may become defiant to avoid confronting these overwhelming feelings; others may use minimization and denial.

When teens become defiant and resistant in therapy, they may provoke your countertransference issues. You may find yourself reacting with anger. It is important to recognize your own feelings so that you do not allow them to interfere with the therapeutic process. Teens need lots of empathy, encouragement, and support during this potentially difficult time.

Ages: This activity is designed for adolescents of all ages.

Materials Needed: Activity sheet and pencils.

Instructions: Instruct the teen to first think about the person or people with whom he or she feels safe.

Ask the teen to write about a person that has never hurt him or her and who can be trusted with difficult secrets. If more than one person can be identified, encourage him or her to include all of these people. Next, have the teen write an essay about sharing a difficult secret with that person or persons.

Processing: After the essay is completed, have the teen read it aloud. We have found it helpful to follow up with queries such as "Tell me about the person/people," "What makes you feel safe with this person/these people?" "Are there any people with whom you don't feel safe? Tell me about them," and "What is your difficult secret?"

The following case example illustrates how one abused teenage girl worked through this activity.

Case Example: *Elisa*

Brief Case History: Elisa was a 14-year-old Hispanic girl who was referred to individual therapy by her primary physician. This referral came after several appointments with her doctor during which she had complaints of stomach pain, a lack of motivation and/or energy, and sleeping all day. The primary physician was concerned with depression and possible drug use secondary to the depression.

Elisa was very difficult to engage in therapy. She was hesitant to disclose anything about herself, her family, or what she was doing in her life. Eventually she did seem to engage more willingly in therapy and began to "open up." Elisa had briefly touched on her hurt and angry feelings regarding her father's alcoholism, her parents' divorce, the multiple "father figures" that she had over the past few years, and the lack of her mother's involvement in her life. However, even after several months of weekly sessions it still seemed as though Elisa was holding something back.

The session began with a discussion of Elisa's poor attendance in school over the last few weeks and her mother's concerns with her failing grades. Following this discussion, Elisa was asked to complete the activity (Activity #33) by writing about a "difficult" secret. Initially, she was extremely resistant to begin the activity. However, with some encouragement and reassurance that she could write about anything that she wanted, she did begin working. After approximately 10 to 15 minutes, Elisa began crying.

Therapist Elisa, what's wrong? What is coming up for you right now?

Elisa Nothing. I don't really want to talk about it.

T But that's the problem, Elisa, you have these feelings inside and you don't want to talk about them. Look where that is getting you. You continue to have stomach problems, you don't want to go to school, your mom is upset about your grades and on your back. It seems like it might be a good thing to start dealing with these feelings. Maybe your life could get better.

E Well it's just so hard to talk about, and I don't want you to be mad at me.

T Elisa, I would never get mad at you because of your feelings.

E It's not my feelings I'm worried about, it's what I did.

T Whatever it is, I'm sure we can work through it. My job is not to make judgments, my job is to help people work their problems out.

(long pause)

E Well, you know how I've been missing a lot of school and how I've been saying it's because I've been sick?

T Yeah.

E Well, its more than that. I had an abortion. I had an abortion when I was 5½ months pregnant. And what am I going to do now? What is God going to do? I will never be forgiven. My mom says it's not on me, it's on her. . . . She is the one who made me have the abortion. . . . And the reason I don't want to go to school is that some of the kids know and they give me a hard time. . . .

The session continued with Elisa pouring out months' and years' worth of history, events, and feelings. This information came forth almost in a stream of consciousness. She proceeded to discuss how she had been molested by more than one of her mother's boyfriends, how she frequently felt neglected by her mother, how she did not feel supported, and how her parents would engage in horrible screaming and hitting fights.

Clinical Impressions: It is not surprising that Elisa took her time in developing a trusting relationship with her therapist. The lack of consistent parental support had left her feeling that she had no one to confide in as well as not knowing who to trust. Given the warm, supportive nature of the therapeutic alliance, Elisa did eventually open up to her therapist about the most difficult secret she was hiding. She was also able to process feelings regarding the various molestations by her mother's boyfriends, her father's alcoholism, and her mother's lack of nurturing.

This case illustrates the need for individual therapy with girls such as Elisa. If Elisa could continue to use her individual sessions in an increasingly open manner, she could progress to joining group therapy, where she would gain peer support. This could be a transition to building positive peer relations outside of therapy.

❑   **Activity #34: Secrets Make Me Feel . . .**

Objective: To express feelings associated with secrets.

This activity is designed to allow the teen to express feelings associated with his or her secrets. The teen may find this activity threatening because breaking the "code of silence" can be such an overwhelming task.

This activity may elicit a great deal of emotions, or you may find the teen completely shut down, denying any feelings or secrets. If the teen is in denial, encourage him or her to discuss what he or she might feel if he or she actually had a secret.

Ages: This activity is designed for adolescents of all ages.

Materials Needed: Activity sheet and pencils.

Instructions: Instruct the teen to think about his or her "secrets" and to be aware of any associated feelings. Then tell the teen to write an essay about his or her feelings connected with secrets.

Processing: After the teen has finished the essay, have him or her read it aloud. It is important to process the essay. We have found it helpful to ask questions such as "How do you feel about your essay?" "Is your secret safe or unsafe? Why?" and "Can you tell me about the secret(s) you thought about?"

It is also important to process with the teen any feelings associated with sharing his or her secrets.

7

Nightmares and Memories

For many victims of abuse, remembering may be the first step toward healing. This may be the most difficult step in the recovery process because many abusive experiences happen at the preverbal stage or at the beginning stages of language acquisition. These children had no way of verbalizing, understanding, or making sense of what was happening to them. If the adolescent victim was preverbal when the abuse occurred, memory of the event(s) may be fragmented or forgotten.

Children who are traumatized prior to their ability to form narrative memories often play out these memories and often fear trauma-related stimuli (Terr, 1994). This can be seen in the play of abused children. As adolescents, they may act out similar scenarios with their peers. For instance, the little girl who used to tie up her Barbie dolls may find herself a victim of aggressive sexual behavior.

Children are born with basic instincts and needs, such as sucking, touching, and being held. They are unable to distinguish between appropriate and inappropriate behaviors. Therefore, when others victimize them, they are unable to label the behavior as abusive.

Obviously, this makes it difficult to help children uncover and work through their experiences. As the child moves into adolescence with this entrenched belief system, puberty further complicates the picture. The normal need for intimacy and nurturance can prove distressful to the abused adolescent because these needs can be confused with feelings associated with past sexual trauma.

In addition to the difficulty of working through preverbal experiences, some children may "block" or repress memories. Repression or dissociation is a coping mechanism that occurs when an individual unconsciously avoids anxiety and distress associated with painful memories (Briere, 1992; Briere & Conte, 1993).

Whereas the capacity for storage of memory is almost limitless, the retrieval can be difficult, especially if the memory is painful. Due to the nature of memory retrieval, many researchers have suggested that children's memories are "suggestible"; others have found children's memories to be quite resilient (Doris, 1991). Some have set forth the notion of a "false memory syndrome" (no such proven syndrome) as an explanation for recovered memories. This debate has created quite a controversy within the mental health field (Karp, 1995). Due to this controversy, the American Professional Society on the Abuse of Children (APSAC, 1992) published a special issue of the *Advisor* that focused on child and adult memories.

Terr (1994) stressed that conflict is the key to repression. Many trauma victims are unwilling or unable to accept that someone they trusted has abused them. Gil (1991) described dissociation as "a process of separating, segregating, and isolating chunks of information, perceptions, memories, motivations, and affects" (p. 22).

There may also be a feeling of danger associated with exposing the perpetrator(s). Some adolescents may still be living with or near the perpetrator(s). Others may have been threatened with frightening consequences if they revealed the abuse. Thus, these victims may consciously deny, block, or suppress the memory as a survival mechanism.

Dreams can be one vehicle to help uncover repressed or blocked memories. As Gil (1991) pointed out, it is believed that dreams are an individual's way of allowing unresolved traumas to leak into consciousness. Dreams may also allow the individual to rehearse things to come. Therefore, sharing dreams and nightmares is a useful, nonthreatening, and nondirective means of working through abusive memories.

It is important to keep in mind that dreams and nightmares can be somewhat distorted aspects of reality. However, over time, bits of the dreams may fit together, much like pieces of a puzzle, helping the individual to remember abusive experiences.

When children or adolescents draw or relate characters in their dreams or fears, they often talk about "monsters." Therefore, it is important to have them confront their monsters. Confrontation can create a sense of empowerment and control over fears, allowing the individual to work through memories more easily.

There are several goals for this chapter. First of all, it is important to remember that working through abuse is a long-term process. This chapter is the beginning point of retrieving and working through memories. There is no "right" or "wrong" way to do this.

One goal is to assist in the process of remembering the abuse. Terr (1994) pointed out that dreams are important to trauma but are not always connected to trauma. Individuals do not necessarily dream about their particular trauma. However, some people who have repressed their trauma do dream about certain aspects of the trauma, particularly as their memories begin to come back toward the surface. Terr (1994) pointed out that many never dream about their traumas. Repeated dreams seem, in particular, to be connected to terrifying experiences derived from actual, outside events (Terr, 1990).

The activities in this chapter are designed to assist the teen in gaining mastery through processing the memories and nightmares so common to many abuse victims. As the individual begins to "unlock" the secrets associated with the abuse, memories will begin to emerge. These memories may surface in many forms. The person may experience nightmares, recurring dreams, or flashbacks. This may be a particularly difficult and frightening period in treatment.

This is a very painful point in the recovery process, and therefore, can be an intense experience for the therapist, both personally and professionally (see "Therapist Issues" in this book's introduction). It is important for you, as the therapist, to remember that the goal is to help guide the teen through his or her thoughts and feelings so as to gain a sense of empowerment. This sense of personal control leads to a healthier sense of self.

One method of gaining mastery over fears is to utilize a technique discussed by Mills and Crowley (1986) in their book *Therapeutic Metaphors for Children and the Child Within* as well as in *Cartoon Magic* (Crowley & Mills, 1989). Although these activities are designed for younger children, they do have some utility for adolescents, especially the more regressed teen. The authors suggested having the child identify a favorite cartoon friend who can help him or her and then to create a cartoon series in which the superhero helps the victim battle the monster. We have included an activity that is adapted to adolescents.

Because this can be such an intense or emotionally charged stage of recovery, you may find it necessary to consult with a colleague to work through your own countertransference issues (Gil & Johnson, 1993). This is a time when you may be getting many phone calls from caretakers, teachers, and other concerned adults regarding the adolescent's behavior and their concerns over how to assist. Although this is a difficult time for the therapist and teen, it is necessary and can be a pivotal point in recovery.

The following activities are designed to assist in exploring and working through difficult and painful memories and scary nightmares or bad dreams. A few case studies have been included to clarify how some of these activities have been used in actual therapy situations. We have provided a brief case history, an example of dialogue between the therapist and teen during the activity, and clinical impressions.

As we have stated in previous chapters, the *Activity Book* includes a section entitled "Teen Talk." You should have the teen read his or her copy before working on the activities. It provides a brief introduction to the concepts covered in this chapter.

❏ **Activity #35: I Had a Dream**

Objective: To begin looking at and processing dreams.

This activity is designed to introduce the adolescent to the concept of exploring dreams. This first activity is set up so that there is no expectation of what kind of dream may be explored. The idea is to just introduce the teen to writing and drawing about dreams, whether the dreams are happy, sad, or scary.

As stated previously, dreams can be a nondirective vehicle to explore unresolved trauma. However, before unresolved trauma is addressed, a less threatening dream may be a good place to start. This could be a scary dream, but it could also be a dream of a funny movie or delightful experience the teen has had.

Ages: This activity is designed for teens of all ages.

Materials Needed: Activity sheet and pencil, crayons, markers, and/ or colored pencils.

Instructions: Instruct the teen to write about a dream he or she has had. Then have the teen pick the most vivid part of his or her dream and draw a picture of it.

Processing: After the activity is completed, have the teen read his or her dream aloud. Then discuss both the dream and the picture. We have found it helpful to follow up with queries such as "Tell me about your dream," "How does this dream make you feel?" "Why?" "How did you feel while you were drawing your dream?" "Why did you pick this dream to write about?" and "Why did you pick this part of your dream to draw?"

❑ **Activity #36: My Scary Dream**

Objective: To process feelings associated with scary dreams.

This activity is designed to help the adolescent explore dreams that have been frightening. With the onslaught of more explicit movies, television, and other products of mass media, children and adolescents have been exposed to stimuli that may result in "bad dreams." As children, adolescents were exposed to storybooks that talked all about children's experiences with bad dreams, monsters (in their closets), and nightmares. Therefore, this activity will most likely be familiar and something the teen will feel comfortable doing.

Ages: This activity is designed for adolescents of all ages, as long as they are able to connect feelings with dreams.

Materials Needed: Activity sheet, pencil, and crayons, colored pencils, and/or markers.

Instructions: Instruct the teen to write about and draw a picture of a dream that made him or her feel scared.

Note: If the teen is resistant or says he or she cannot recall a scary dream, instruct him or her to focus on something that creates scary feelings rather than drawing a picture of a dream.

Processing: After the teen has completed the activity, have him or her read the dream aloud. Then discuss both the dream and the picture. We have found it helpful to follow up with queries such as "Tell me about your scary dream," "What makes this dream scary to you?" "Have you had other dreams that are frightening? Tell me about them," and "Tell me about your drawing."

❏ **Activity #37: The Never-Ending Dream**

Objective: To explore dreams that are recurring.

This activity is designed to encourage the teen to explore dreams that are recurring. Recurring dreams can be extremely valuable in terms of treatment. As previously stated, dreams can be the roadway into unresolved trauma. Thus, recurring dreams tend to be significant in that they may serve as a "red flag" that the individual is attempting to resolve some internal conflict.

Recurring dreams can also serve another important function in therapy. They can be used as yardsticks to measure progress in terms of internal resolution. You may find that over time the recurring dream changes. It is important to monitor the changes, focusing on mastery and empowerment.

This activity is designed for teens who have had recurring dreams. It can be very powerful. Obviously, if a teen has not experienced a recurring dream, this activity may be skipped.

Ages: Adolescents of all ages should be able to participate in this activity as long as they have experienced recurring dreams.

Materials Needed: Activity sheet, pencil, and crayons, colored pencils, and/or markers.

Instructions: Instruct the teen to think about a dream which he or she has had more than once. Then have the teen write about the recurring dream. Once this is completed, have the teen draw a picture depicting this dream.

Processing: After the activity is completed, have the teen discuss the dream and the picture. We have found it helpful to follow up with queries such as "Tell me about the dream you keep having," "How does this dream make you feel?" "How did it feel to draw this picture?" and "How would you like to change your dream?"

❏ Activity #38: The Monster in My Dream

Objective: To begin looking at various "monsters" that are found in dreams and other places.

This activity is designed to allow the teen to begin to confront any "monsters" they may have feared. Often, children who have been abused talk about "monsters." They may not initially connect these "monsters" with their abuse history. However, as they progress in therapy, these children often begin to talk about the "monster" who hurt them as they become empowered to face their abuse. Because many abused adolescents were first victimized as younger children, this activity may require them to remember a dream they had as children.

In her art therapy book *Breaking the Silence* (1990), Malchiodi described a common feature of the artwork of children of battered women. The metaphor depicted in their drawings was of a monster of some sort. Although children in general seem to enjoy drawing monsters, the monster appears to take on more metaphorical significance in the drawings of children from violent homes or children who have been abused. Often these children explicitly or implicitly link the monster with their abuser, or with their own feelings of pain, anger, fear, or loneliness. According to Malchiodi, "These are the invisible monsters that gnaw away at the inner self, creatures that destroy self-esteem and leave in their wake anxiety and pain. For children from violent homes, the monsters can be an abusive parent, neglect, incest, and severe emotional trauma" (p. 4).

Adolescents may approach this activity from many different perspectives, according to where they are in their own recovery program and where they are emotionally. If the teen is rather disconnected from his or her feelings, the drawing may become merely an art exercise. However, if the teen is at all connected to the trauma of the abuse, he or she may experience a tremendous amount of stress and anxiety while engaging in this activity. As the therapist, it is important for you to attend to the teen's reactions as he or she embarks on this activity.

Ages: This activity is designed for adolescents of all ages.

Materials Needed: Activity sheet and pencils, crayons, colored pencils, and/or markers.

Instructions: Instruct the teen to draw a picture of his or her "monster."

Processing: After the teen has completed his or her drawing, it is important to follow up with queries such as "Tell me about your monster," "How did you feel when you drew your monster?" and "Tell me about your feelings."

The following case example illustrates how one abused teen processed this activity.

Case Example: *Jennifer*

Brief Case History: Jennifer, a 14-year-old Caucasian girl, was a member of an adolescent girls' trauma recovery group at a family service
agency. She had been referred to group after spending 3 months in a
residential treatment center (RTC) where she had primarily worked
on anger management. Jennifer had been physically abused by her
stepfather for several years (ages 8-13), and she had been raped by her
boyfriend just prior to her RTC placement. Jennifer's physical assaultiveness had been escalating to the point that she had threatened a girl
at school with a knife. She had also smashed almost all the breakable
items in her family's home by the time the police arrived.

At the RTC, her behavior had markedly improved, and now,
instead of being openly angry, she was using sarcasm and jokes to
express her anger. Although this was viewed as better than hurting
others physically, it seemed as if Jennifer's anger had gone "under-
ground" and become more covert. Her parents continued to deny
that the stepfather had ever beaten her, and they professed not to
believe Jennifer's story of the rape. In her outpatient therapy group,
Jennifer was well liked by her peers. She always had something funny
to say to get them off the hook when being confronted by the therapist
at a crucial point. Jennifer would sulk and withdraw when this behavior was pointed out to her. Sometimes Jennifer would start discussing
her own issues in a serious manner, displaying excellent insight; then
all of a sudden, she would make a very tangential remark, switching
the entire focus of the discussion. The therapist decided to have the
group participate in a nonverbal activity in an effort to circumvent
Jennifer's defense of playing word games.

The group was asked to draw a picture of a frightening image or
"monster" that they might have encountered in their dreams or
other places. Although Jennifer joked, "You mean I can have my very
own monster?", once she started drawing, she put a lot of time and
effort into this drawing (see Illustration 7.1).

Out of all her peers, Jennifer was the last to finish. The following dialogue took place as Jennifer was asked to share her drawing with the group.

Therapist So, Jennifer, tell us about your "monster."

Jennifer Well, first of all, he's male—and he's me! (Looks around for a reaction from peers, who just stare at her)

T Hmm . . . so you're a monster and you're a male too. . . . Tell us more about the drawing.

J See the horns? He's very well defended. Everyone's scared of him. People aren't used to seeing a purple monster on the street! (laughs)

Peer Come on, you really think this is you?

J Well, yeah. . . . Everyone always tells me how bad and mean I am . . . so I'll just satisfy them by being my own monster!

Peer So then why do you have to be a guy?

J I don't know. . . . Maybe this picture is really my stepfather and that asshole who raped me. . . . Hey! I can be them, too!

Peer You're confusing me.

T: It does get confusing when you're angry at the people who hurt you and you don't know what to do with that hurt and anger. Sometimes we act it out on others, and sometimes we feel as if we are bad people ourselves.

J Whatever. . . . I'm going to put this on my bedroom door and scare everybody with how ugly I am! (laughs)

Clinical Impressions: Jennifer showed good insight when she identified her "monster" as her stepfather and as her rapist. She also knew that her hurt and anger had turned her into some kind of "monster" as well, capable of alienating others. She saw her anger as ugly and as male, at once identifying with it and rejecting it. This put Jennifer in a precarious position in that she denigrated her own feelings and perceptions and used what she did not truly want (the "monster") to protect herself.

The challenge for Jennifer was to accept her reality even if her parents never believed in or supported her. She also had to find ways to express her anger that did not involve assaulting and threatening others and being verbally abusive. It appeared that drawing and other nonverbal modalities would be an effective way for Jennifer to process these challenges.

❑ Activity #39: Cartoon Superhero

Objective: To explore fears by invoking the aid of a cartoon superhero.

This activity is designed to begin the problem-solving and empowerment process. After the teen has identified his or her monster, the next step is to begin mastering the fears associated with it. As stated earlier, utilizing "cartoon friends" can be a powerful technique in helping to resolve fear associated with trauma (Crowley & Mills, 1989).

Many teens love cartoons and superheroes. This can be an excellent medium in which to engage the teen. Drawing cartoons allows individuals to have fun and find humor while providing powerful symbolism. Thus, cartoons become metaphoric symbols, allowing teens to "walk through the trauma" and gain a sense of empowerment.

We realize that this activity alone will not resolve the trauma. It will begin the process of mastering difficult experiences. This activity is structured so that teens can identify a cartoon "helper" that can help a younger child deal with problems. By distancing themselves from the character who is the victom (small child), they can feel less threatened. It is hoped that through processing this activity, they will be able to identify with the superhero who helps the kid. This is an indirect way to have teens begin to see themselves as stronger people who are capable of handling problems.

Ages: Adolescents of all ages should have no problem identifying a cartoon character that symbolizes "the hero" who can help solve problems.

Materials Needed: Activity sheet and pencils, crayons, colored pencils, and/or markers.

Instructions: Instruct the teen to draw a cartoon of a superhero-type character that can help a younger child with a problem.

Processing: After the teen has drawn the cartoon superhero, it would be helpful to follow up with queries such as "Tell me about the cartoon superhero," "What can the superhero do to help younger kids with their problems?" and "How do you think younger kids would feel if they had a special superhero? Why?"

Note: It is possible that some teens may identify more with the kid ("victim") needing help than with the superhero. If this happens, processing with the teen may include questions such as "How do you think the kid felt to have someone else to depend on?" and "If you were the kid, how would you like someone more powerful to help you with your problems?"

The following case example will illustrate how one abused teen processed this activity.

Case Example: *Jose*

Brief Case History: Jose was a 13-year-old Mexican American teen who was living with his maternal grandmother when he entered individual therapy. He had been living with his grandmother for approximately 3½ years. He was placed with her following a brief stay in a shelter after his mother was arrested for cocaine possession with the intent to sell. Jose's father was also in prison; his conviction was connected with an attempted murder charge. Jose's older brother was living with relatives in another state, and his three younger siblings lived with an aunt.

Jose was referred to therapy by his caseworker (for the State) because he had been getting more and more out of control over the past few years. His grandmother was becoming concerned with his anger level and ultimately feared that she would need to return him to the State's custody if he continued to become so easily angered. Jose was frequently being sent to the office for disciplinary action while he was at school. In addition, his negative behaviors were

escalating at home. He had gotten to the point where he was beginning to throw things and had even put a hole through the wall.

Once in therapy, Jose began to share some of his past history, but
it seemed very difficult for him to open up and disclose many
details. Eventually he began to attend group sessions in addition to
his individual therapy. It was in the individual therapy setting that
he was able to really explore his past and begin to address the
trauma that he had endured through most of his growing years. It
seemed that Jose had not only been the victim of frequent beatings
by his father but had been forced to watch his mother and siblings
receive the same torturous treatment. This continued from the time
Jose was born until he was 8 years old, when his father was put into
prison on attempted murder charges. It seemed that his father had
been caught in a drug deal gone bad.

Building rapport with Jose was fairly easy as he had developed
strong relationships with his mother and grandmother in his earlier
years. Thus, establishing "trust" with a woman seemed fairly easy
for him. It was not until he moved into the exploration of trauma
that his recovery became more difficult. It turned out that exploring
his trauma through the use of art was extremely useful for Jose.
Therefore, Activity #39, "Cartoon Superhero," was introduced as a
vehicle to help Jose portray a superhero who could help kids with
their problems. The session began with a discussion of Jose's favorite cartoon and superheroes. Jose was not able to identify any
superhero character as a helper to younger children. He did, however, identify "Speedy Gonzales" as someone who would be able to
help and was able to explain why this was his choice.

Therapist Jose, tell me why you think Speedy Gonzales would be
   able to help kids when they were in trouble.
Jose He could help because he is very fast.
T Fast—how is that going to help kids in trouble?
J He is so fast that he could zoom in, grab the kid before he could
   get hit or anything, and then zoom back out. He is so fast he
   could even come back if anyone else needed help before they
   could get hurt.
T Yeah, he is very fast.

The rest of the session was spent processing how Jose's father would start getting out of control and how Jose would frequently wish that someone or something would rush in and stop him.

Clinical Impressions: Clearly, art is a powerful tool in Jose's therapy. Through discussing how Speedy Gonzales could rescue a child before he got hurt, Jose was able to express his own need for rescue in a nonthreatening manner. Jose was able to conceive of a benevolent male figure who rescues people instead of beating them up. Hopefully, Jose will use this as a role model for his own life.

Future therapy sessions will need to address the impact of the constant family disruption and domestic violence. At this point in Jose's life, he seems to have identified with his father in handling stresses in a violent manner. This needs to be explored. Perhaps he can come to see Speedy Gonzales as a more positive image to emulate.

❏ **Activity #40: Superhero to the Rescue!**

Objective: To explore a variety of ways that a superhero can assist in problem solving.

This activity is designed to continue the problem-solving process, allowing the teen to explore a variety of ways that a "superhero" could assist in solving problems. This activity is also intended to allow the teen to practice a technique that can be used at home.

Ages: This activity is designed for adolescents of all ages.

Materials Needed: Activity sheet; pencils, crayons, colored pencils, and/or markers; and additional paper if needed.

Instructions: Instruct the teen to draw a cartoon strip depicting a superhero helping kids with their problems. The teen can draw as many frames as he or she wants to complete the cartoon strip. It may be helpful to bring in the cartoon section from your local paper as an example to assist in this project.

Processing: After the teen has completed this activity, it is important to discuss it with him or her by following up with queries such as "Tell me about your cartoon strip," "How does it feel to have a superhero help the kid with his or her problems? Why?" and "How do you think it would feel to be able to solve problems like the superhero? Why?" "What do you think the kid in your cartoon feels like?"

❑ **Activity #41: Significant Memories**

Objective: To process various important memories that create certain feelings.

This activity is designed to assist the teen in exploring various important memories in his or her life. It is also intended to allow the adolescent to practice expressing his or her memories, linking up thoughts and feelings with particular memories.

The teen will be asked to explore his or her first memory, as well as his or her best, saddest, and scariest memories. Because exploring can be an extremely difficult task, the teen is first asked to start with the less threatening memories, such as the first and best memories. The teen is then asked to get in touch with more difficult, sad, and frightening memories.

It is important to monitor closely for any signs of regression, such as self-mutilating behavior, that may occur at this stage of recovery. As difficult memories are explored, the teen may begin cutting on him or herself or engaging in other self-destructive behavior. Some teens describe this as a way to actually "feel" something as opposed to being "numb." Others may use this as a way to self-punish, and still others may use it as a way to draw attention to their inner pain.

Ages: This activity is designed for adolescents of all ages.

Materials Needed: Activity sheets and pencil.

Instructions: Instruct the teen to write an essay about his or her various memories listed on each page.

Processing: After the teen has completed writing, have him or her read the essays aloud. It is important to discuss the feelings associated with that particular memory. We have found it helpful to follow up with queries such as "Tell me about your memories," "What was your first memory all about? How did you feel about this memory?" "What were your best, saddest, and scariest memories all about?" "How did you feel as you wrote about these memories?" and "Which memory was the most comfortable to write about, and which one was the most uncomfortable? Why?"

❏ **Activity #42: Memory Box**

Objective: To make a box for things that are reminders of difficult memories and to collect various items for the memory box.

The first step of this activity is designed to provide a special place to put things that remind the teen of difficult memories. This may include pictures of dreams or "monsters." For many teens, this is a fun activity that encourages creativity and empowerment. They are in charge of designing something that will allow them to feel that the memories are contained. Some teens will also want to use locks to ensure that the boxes are safeguarded.

The second step of this activity is designed to give teens the opportunity to continue working through various significant memories. Whereas the previous activities were more structured and focused on writing and drawing, this activity encourages teens to explore and express important memories, using their unique and individual representations for past experiences. It is important to allow teens to choose anything that represents their memories, such as pictures or objects.

This may be a difficult time in the healing process in that teens often regress when they confront painful memories. They may even feel "out of control." Making a special place to contain these painful memories can be beneficial to the healing process in that it provides a safe structure in which teens can contain their thoughts and feelings. This may allow these teens to feel more "in control."

Ages: Adolescents of all ages should have no problems with this activity. The sophistication of the final product created by the individual will depend on his or her developmental age.

Materials Needed: Crayons, colored pencils, and/or markers, boxes, glue, scissors, and other art and craft supplies that encourage creativity. Also needed are found objects, pictures, magazines, photographs, and various other items that the teen may associate with memories.

Instructions:
    Step 1: Instruct the teen to think about how he or she would like to decorate a box to be used to keep his or her memories safe. Then give the teen various sizes of boxes to choose from and ask him or her to choose the kind of box that is needed for his or her memories. Once the box has been chosen, instruct the teen to decorate it, using the supplies provided.
    Step 2: Instruct the teen to begin collecting things for the memory box. This may include looking through various magazines and gathering photographs and other found objects. Then, instruct the teen to cut out the pictures and pick other items to place in the memory box.
    This activity may take more than one session. Therefore, you may tell the teen to look for various objects that he or she would like to include in his or her memory box in between sessions.

Processing: After the teen has completed his or her box, it is important to process the activity by following up with queries such as "Tell me about your box" and "How did you feel while you were decorating your box?"
    After the teen has collected the items necessary for his or her memory box, it is important to discuss all the items collected. We have found it helpful to give prompts such as "Tell me about what

you have chosen to put in your memory box. Why did you pick each one?" "How did you feel while going through the process of selecting the stuff you collected for your memory box?" and "Tell me about your feelings and the memories that go with each object you chose."

PHASE III

Repairing the Sense of Self

8

Letting Go of Guilt and Shame

Although the focus in this book is on the abused adolescent, many of these teens first suffered their abuse in early childhood. As stated in our last book, *Treatment Strategies for Abused Children* (Karp & Butler, 1996):

> Developmentally, young children are at a stage where they are naturally egocentric, seeing the world from their perspective and assuming others see it the same way. As a result of this unrealistic point of view, they many times mistakenly take on the responsibility for others' actions even those that have been abusive. (p. 163)

Briere (1992) and Everstine and Everstine (1989) addressed an important point that when the abuser shifts the blame to the child, the child experiences intense feelings of guilt for the abuse. When this occurs in early childhood and is not dealt with, it becomes entrenched in the child's sense of self. As adolescents, this damaged sense of self is filled with intense guilt and shame over the abusive experience(s).

There are many other reasons why adolescents tend to blame themselves. They may have been told that the abuse was their fault, or their religious beliefs may inadvertently support the idea that sexual experience outside of wedlock is a sin, so that they see themselves as participating in a sinful act. In addition, as pointed out in Chapter 1, the normal sexual development of adolescents going through puberty compounds the confusion. Normal sexual urges can become confusing when the teen is approached by an older adult person. The issue of power and control can be quite perplexing to teens since they want to feel that they are "in control."

If the abuse occurred with a member of the immediate family, the teen seems to take on more responsibility for the abuse. At times, the daughter in an incestuous relationship may even see herself as a willing participant. She may fear a breakup of the family system or want to protect one parent from the hurt that knowledge of the incest would bring. Therefore, there may be added pressure to keep the incest or physical abuse a family secret (Briere, 1992).

In addition, adolescents may experience self-blame for the abuse because they think they should have done something to make it stop. They are not able to understand the reality of just how powerless they truly are. As stated previously, they feel as if they are "old enough" to make their own decisions. They are unaware of the magnitude of the imbalance of power in the relationship. Unfortunately, the adults or other family members around them frequently contribute to this faulty belief by blaming them for the abuse. This only adds and compounds to the self-imposed guilt and shame already felt.

Young children and adolescents have a basic need for nurturing. When this need is not met, they will accept any form of closeness, including sexual touching or even physically harsh treatment. At times, sexual molestation physically feels good, which only serves to intensify the confusion. It is easy to see how this leads to more guilt and shame and the resultant self-hatred.

Before individuals can let go of guilt and shame, they must first recognize it, verbalize it, and defuse the power that lies behind it. Admitting shame is the first step in that direction. Secrecy breeds shame. Therefore, as was discussed in previous chapters, it is critical to develop a trusting relationship so that secrets can be shared. This will enable the teen to emerge from under the cloak of guilt and shame and begin caring for the "child within."

Once the power behind guilt and shame is diffused, the next step is to begin the process of grieving and mourning over losses. Often teens experience the sense that they have lost the essence of childhood. However, due to their lack of life experiences, they do not fully realize what they have lost. This is a critical time in the healing process.

The goal of this chapter is to assist the teen in letting go of guilt and shame, which is at the core of the damaged self. This is probably the most difficult aspect of the healing process. Before the individual can truly emerge into a healthy survivor, he or she must let go of the shame, feel the pain, and grieve over the losses. Completing this process allows the disintegrated self to integrate and take shape. Gil (1996) describes this process, utilizing a metaphor of a shattered mirror. She comments that, "the shattered mirror represents a traumatic event for a youngster . . . . The event is overwhelming and therefore cannot be easily reassembled and assimilated." (p. 141)

The activities in this chapter will assist in addressing the "core" issues that have created a damaged sense of self. As previously stated, the abused adolescent typically feels responsible for the abuse and harbors enormous feelings of guilt and shame. This can be a trying period in the therapeutic process because the teen typically is entrenched and invested in his or her unhealthy beliefs regarding a sense of responsibility for the abuse. The psychological position of the victim may appear intractable. You may feel as if you are on an emotional rollercoaster as the teen goes through a "push-pull" process in letting go of guilt and shame feelings.

As provided in previous chapters, this chapter contains case studies to assist you in further understanding how some of these activities have been used in actual therapy situations. We have provided a brief case history, an example of dialogue during the activity, and clinical impressions.

You should have the adolescent read the section "Teen Talk" for this chapter in their copy of the *Activity Book*. We have found that reading "Teen Talk" before beginning the activities is informative for the therapist as well. This will give a brief introduction to this chapter and a description of the goals.

❏ Activity #43: Jared's Story

Objective: To begin working on feelings associated with abuse, such as guilt and shame.

This activity is designed to introduce the concept of self-blame, so commonly felt by abused children and adolescents. As previously stated, stories are a less threatening medium and can facilitate discussions of difficult feelings. Abused teens often assume the burden of responsibility for their abuse and may harbor enormous feelings of guilt and shame. This story will help adolescents who are dealing with guilt and shame associated with disclosure of past abuse. It may also elicit feelings directly associated with the actual abusive experience.

This story may very well stir up a variety of emotions, central of which is shame. It is very important for the teen to realize that he or she can process the feelings of guilt and shame so that the healing process can proceed. This is a difficult process because children and adolescents really hold on to the belief that they are responsible for the abusive experiences. Unfortunately, this concept is too often reinforced by those who continue to doubt child sexual abuse.

Ages: This activity is appropriate for adolescents of all ages. This story may be read aloud to the academically challenged individual or read aloud to the group if you are working in a group setting.

Materials Needed: Activity sheet and pencil.

Instructions: Instruct the teen to read or listen to Jared's story. After the reading of the story, instruct him or her to complete the questions related to the story.

Processing: After the adolescent has finished the story, it is important to follow up with a discussion. We have found it helpful to ask questions such as "What do you think about the story?" "How did Jared feel in the story? Why?" "Do you think it was Jared's fault? Why or why not?" and "Have you ever felt like Jared? When? Why?"

❑ **Activity #44: My Story**

Objective: To write about the abusive experiences and compile them into a book.

This activity is designed to encourage the adolescent to confront the people who hurt him or her by writing and illustrating an account of abusive experiences and putting it into book form. Because the teen has already been talking about secrets and memories, the next logical step is putting it all together in a book format. Calling this activity "My Story" gives teens an opportunity to express their story from their own perspective, thus giving them back some of the power they lost when they were placed in a victim role.

Ages: This activity is appropriate for adolescents of all ages, however, the academically challenged teen may need assistance.

Materials Needed: Drawing/construction paper; pencils, crayons, markers, and/or colored pencils; extra paper; paper fasteners; string or cord.

Instructions: Instruct the teen to think about his or her abusive past and identify the people responsible for the abuse. Have him or her list them on the page provided in the *Activity Book.* Then, tell the teen to write about and illustrate various abusive experiences from their past. If the teen has had multiple perpetrators, it may be easier to focus on one perpetrator at a time when writing.

Once the story is completed, it is important to read it together. Some teens may be resistant to reading the story aloud. It may be necessary to give the teen an option of just having you read it silently. After the story is reviewed, have the teen design a cover for the book. The final step is to put all of the pages together, including the front and back covers. You can use paper fasteners, string, or cord to bind the book.

Note: The academically challenged teen may need more assistance from the therapist regarding direction, dictation, and organization of the book.

Processing: After the teen has completed his or her book, it is important to go through the entire book and process it by following up with queries such as "Tell me about your book," "What did it feel like telling your story?" and "How do you feel putting your story in a book? Why?"

❑ **Activity #45: I Would Say . . .**

Objective: To confront the abuser(s) by means of writing a statement to each perpetrator identified in the abuse book created in Activity #44.

This activity is designed to begin the process of addressing the teen's response to his or her abuse. It is important for individuals to confront the abuser(s) and express thoughts and feelings associated with the abuse, as well as making statements directed toward the person(s) responsible. However, it is not necessary for individuals to *personally* or *physically* confront the abuser(s).

This may be difficult for some people to do, while others will use it as an opportunity to gain "power" by exaggerating and inflating their responses. For example, some teens may state things such as "I'll kill you if you ever hurt me again" and may get very detailed on how they would accomplish this.

It is important for you, as the therapist, to understand that this is just the teen's way of attempting to gain power that was taken from him or her by the abuser. The teen is attempting to move from a sense of powerlessness to a position of having some control. You will need to process the reality of the statements and assist in separating wishes and desires from what is real.

Ages: This activity is appropriate for adolescents who are at a stage, developmentally, where they have enough ego strength to confront the abuser(s) with their feelings.

Materials Needed: Activity sheet and pencil.

Instructions: Instruct the teen to reread his or her story. Some teens may either choose or need you to read it to them. Then, tell the teen to write what he or she would like to say to each perpetrator. It is important to put words in writing because this will assist the teen in expressing intangible feelings in a concrete form. This is another step toward feeling empowered.

Note: Be aware that even teens with moderately stable ego strength may show signs of regression because this exercise taps into their guilt and shame.

After the teen has completed his or her statement to the perpetrator, have him or her read it aloud. It is important to discuss the statements by following up with queries such as "Tell me about your statement(s)," "Is there anything else you want to say to this person? What?" and "How does it feel to express your feelings to the person who hurt you? Why?"

❑ Activity #46: Thinking It Was My Fault

Objective: To begin addressing guilt and shame associated with abuse by looking at self-blame.

Although the adolescent has been introduced to the concept that abuse is not the victim's fault, this is a difficult concept to get across. Therefore, you, as the therapist, will need to address this over and over again.

When adolescents think abuse is their fault, they incorporate guilt and shame feelings around the abuse. They begin to feel intense shame that is difficult to let go of. One place to start is to have the teen begin to address how he or she came to think it was his or her fault. This then allows the teen to confront "faulty thinking" and begins the process of *cognitive restructuring* of faulty thinking or mistaken belief systems.

Ages: This activity is designed for adolescents of all ages.

Instructions: Instruct the teen to read each sentence and complete it, stating why it feels as if the abuse was his or her fault. A discussion of self-blame may be helpful before beginning this activity. A review of "thinking errors" in *The Feeling Good Handbook* (Burns, 1989) may be helpful.

Materials Needed: Activity sheet and pencil.

Processing: After the teen has completed the sentences, it is important to go over each one and discuss the responses. During the processing of this activity, we have found it helpful to ask questions such as "How do you feel about your sentences? Why?" "What does 'fault' mean to you?" and "Was this activity hard or easy for you? Why?"

The following case example will illustrate how one abused pre-teen processed this activity.

Case Example: *Amy*

Brief Case History: Amy's case was discussed in *Treatment Strategies for Abused Children* (Karp & Butler, 1996). Because Amy presented an interesting case history as well as providing a good example for this activity and the next, we decided to use her example again here. Briefly, Amy was a nearly 12-year-old Caucasian girl who had a history of physical, emotional, and sexual abuse by her mother and her numerous boyfriends. During one visit with her mother (while in foster care), Amy was kidnapped by her mother. Amy's mother took her to a different state, changed her name, and dyed her hair. This girl suffered severe trauma due to the abuse and kidnapping. She also went through a disrupted adoption attempt.

This activity was completed after Amy had been in the Child Residential Program for several months. She had been struggling with feelings of guilt, so the therapist decided to use cognitive restructuring in an attempt to help her sort out her feelings. Therefore, Activities #46 and #47 were done in one session. The following dialogue occurred during the discussion of Activity #46.

Therapist Amy, we've talked about how you are always blaming yourself for the times you were hurt.

Amy Yeah.

T I want you to finish these sentences so we can see why you sometimes believe it was your fault. Then we'll talk about it. Okay?

After Amy completed her sentences, she wanted to read them to the therapist.

A Okay. Well, first of all I thought it was my fault because I thought I should have been able to get away from it.

T Okay.

A Number 2, sometimes I believe it was my fault because I thought I deserved it when my Dad slammed me on the chair.

T I think we'll need to talk about these. . . . Go ahead. . . .

A Number 3, sometimes I believe it was my fault because my sister did not believe me when I told her that I was molested by Mom's boyfriend.

T So you blamed yourself for that?

A Yes. Number 4, sometimes I believe it was my fault because when I got taken away from my mom I thought it was my fault—I wasn't good enough.

As soon as Amy finished this paper, the next paper, with Activity #47, was given to her and an explanation of changing her last statements to more positive statements was discussed. Clinical impressions will be given at the end of Activity #47.

❏ Activity #47: It Really Wasn't My Fault!

Objective: To learn a cognitive restructuring technique to counter negative self-statements.

This activity is designed to "piggyback" on the last activity so that the adolescent can follow up with a more reality-based response about why the abuse is not really his or her "fault." This process is also referred to as *cognitive restructuring* (Beck & Emery, 1985). It is very difficult for adolescents to truly believe that their abuse was not their fault; they take responsibility for it just as they often believe that their parents' divorce was their fault.

This activity may take a great deal of discussion before the teen will be able to complete the sentences, depending on his or her sense of responsibility regarding the abuse. The teen needs to process in a more general sense why the abuse was or is not his or her fault before getting to more specific reasons.

Ages: Adolescents of all ages should be able to complete this activity.

Materials Needed: Activity sheet and pencils.

Instructions: After the discussion regarding "fault," instruct the teen to complete the sentences.

Note: It is important to note that usually Activities #46 and #47 are completed together so that teens can see how their negative/faulty thinking can be changed.

Processing: Activities #46 and #47 should be processed together. After the individual has completed these activities, have the sentences read aloud. After reading the sentences, we have found it helpful to ask questions such as "How do you feel about your sentences? Why?" "Why isn't it the victims' fault when they are abused?" and "Was this activity easy or difficult to complete? Why?"

The following example of Activity #47 is a continuation from Activity #46 (see the case example from the previous activity).

Continued Case Example: *Amy*

After Amy completed Activity #46, and after she and the therapist had discussed thinking errors, she was given Activity #47 to complete.

Therapist Amy, now I want you to go back and look at your sentences about how you sometimes think it was your fault. Let's take a good look at each one.

Amy Okay.

T Look at Number 1. Do you really think you could have gotten away? Think of how young you were and how big your mom's boyfriends were.

A I see what you mean. I can change the sentence to how it wasn't my fault.

T Right! How would you change that?

A Well, I was not big. My mom's boyfriends were way too big and too strong for me to get away from them.

T I agree with you. Now that's more like it. I want you to finish the rest of these sentences.

After Amy finished the sentences she wanted to read them aloud.

A Number 2, it was not my fault because my dad should have had his control before hurting me like that. I never deserve being hurt in any way.

T I agree! That's a great way to change your other sentence. Why did you think you deserved it at the time?

A Well, I wasn't listening to him, but I have been learning how to keep my control, and he was an adult. He should know about that.

T Just because you weren't listening to him isn't a reason to hurt you. I'm glad you can see that now.

A Number 3, it was not my fault because my sister did not believe me when I told her about the molestation. I know that it had happened to me. I shouldn't have worried that she didn't believe me. I guess I started wondering if it ever happened, but I know it did.

T I'm glad you're beginning to trust yourself.

A Number 4, it was not my fault because she had lots of chances and blew them to have me in the house with her. I know that I am good. I still miss her, though.

T Of course you do. It's not easy to be taken away from your mother. That's going to be a hard one for you to completely deal with. You talk a lot about wanting to see your mother again.

A Yeah, but then I get really angry and say I don't want to see her again. I get so frustrated.

T I can imagine. How did you feel while you did this activity?

A I felt good about changing my other sentences. I don't really want to blame myself, but sometimes I do.

T Amy, should children be blamed for their abuse?

A No. They're only little. Parents are supposed to take care of their children and protect them. My mom didn't protect me from her boyfriends. That's why she lost me.

Soon after that, the session ended. Amy seemed very proud of herself for how she was able to change her negative, self-blaming sentences into statements about how the things that had happened to her were *not* her fault.

Clinical Impressions: The sentences pretty much reflected how Amy felt about herself at the time she was being abused. Both activities reflected the "push-pull" she went through continually. She defended her mother and then rejected her. She blamed herself for the abuse by her father and then seemed to see "intellectually" that it was not her fault.

Amy is a typical example of a child who has been severely scarred by her traumatic history. She was subjected to an abusive mother whose many boyfriends molested her. In addition, Amy was exposed to her mother's life as a prostitute. Then her mother kidnapped her and changed her name. Following that, she was molested while in foster care. This child did not know whom to trust, for good reason.

The two activities were completed during one session so that Amy would not be left with her faulty thinking. It was decided that it would be better for her to challenge these thinking errors and restructure them into more reality-based cognitions.

Amy responded very well to this approach. She seemed to enjoy the challenge to her "thinking errors" and confirmation that she was not at fault. In fact, a copy was given to her so that whenever she made these statements to herself she could look back and see how to challenge this way of thinking.

This approach of cognitive restructuring will need to be used many times with Amy. It will help her integrate a new belief system into her repertoire so that she will continue to build a stronger and more positive sense of self.

❏ **Activity #48: Me—Before and After**

Objective: To evaluate the damage done to the self by drawing the self before and after being hurt.

This activity is designed to assist adolescents in evaluating how they perceived themselves before and during the abusive period in their life. Some adolescents may take this activity very literally, simply drawing a picture of themselves as a young child and then as a teen. However, for others this can be a deeper, more revealing activity. They may draw a young child looking happy and content and then draw a "damaged" child/adolescent who is quite sad, hurt, or angry. Parts of their body may even look "damaged."

Ages: Adolescents of all ages should be able to complete this activity.

Materials Needed: Activity sheet and pencils, crayons, colored pencils, and/or markers.

Instructions: Instruct the teen to first draw a picture of him- or herself before the abuse happened. Then have the teen draw a picture of the "hurt self."

Processing: After the teen has drawn the "before" and "after" pictures, it is important to discuss the drawings. We have found it helpful to follow up with queries such as "Tell me about the picture of yourself before you were hurt," "How do you feel in this picture? Why?" "Tell me about the picture of your 'hurt self,' " "How do you feel in this picture? Why?" and "How did you feel while drawing each of your pictures? Why?"

❑ Activity #49: "Lost" Things

Objective: To discuss the many losses from abuse.

This activity is designed to allow adolescents to explore the sense of loss that often occurs from abuse. Children and adolescents who have been abused often grow up before their time. They may forget how to play, or they may never have had the opportunity to learn how to play and be a kid.

The losses for some abused children and adolescents may be very evident, as when they are placed in foster homes or put up for adoption, thus losing their biological families. To these individuals, the concept of loss is fairly easy to understand because the loss is so concrete and real. On the other hand, some losses are not so obvious. For example, the "loss of innocence" is difficult for teenagers to understand. Some teens feel they have lost their entire childhood.

Ages: This activity is appropriate for adolescents of all ages.

Materials Needed: Activity sheet and pencils.

Instructions: Before starting this activity, it might be a good idea to have a discussion with the teen regarding the concept of loss as it relates to being abused. It will be important to review things such as feeling "too grown-up" when one was supposed to enjoy being a "kid," the loss of a family if the family has been separated due to the abuse allegations, and the sadness and guilt that may stem from the abuse.

Instruct the teen to think about the things he or she has lost because of the abuse. Then have him or her write down these losses on the activity sheet.

Note: Some adolescents may experience depressive symptoms during this activity due to the intense feelings regarding their losses. It will be important for you to monitor the teen's mood during this stage and adjust the activity so that the teen does not become overwhelmed. You may want to move more slowly through the activities during this stage of the healing process, allowing more time to process.

Processing: After the teen has completed his or her list, have the list read aloud. We have found it helpful to process this activity by following up with queries such as "Tell me about your list of 'lost' things," "Which thing on your list is the hardest for you? Why?" and "How did you feel writing your list? Why?"

❏ **Activity #50: My Letter**

Objective: To learn how to comfort the "hurt child within" by writing a letter to the *hurt child*.

This activity is designed to allow the teen to address the sad and hurt feelings resulting from the abusive experience(s). It is important for adolescents to recognize the "hurt child within" and to validate the child's feelings. One very effective way to address this is to write a therapeutic letter to the "hurt child within."

Writing therapeutic letters has been found to be an excellent way to confront difficult feelings (Bass & Davis, 1988). It allows the child abuse survivor to be more direct in confronting these feelings, rather than just talking "about" these feelings.

Ages: This activity is designed for adolescents of all ages.

Materials Needed: Activity sheet and pencils.

Instructions: Instruct the teen to write a letter to his or her "hurt child." Academically challenged adolescents may need assistance with this activity. They may need to dictate their letter.

Processing: After the adolescent has written his or her letter to the "hurt child," it is important to process the letter by asking questions such as "How did it feel to write your letter? Why?" "Tell me about your 'hurt child,' " and "Is there anything else you would like to add?"

The following case example will illustrate how one trauma victim processed this activity.

Case Example: *Kerrie*

Brief Case History: Kerrie was an 18-year-old Caucasian single mother who was attending a weekly support group for teen mothers and weekly individual therapy. She had been involved in her recovery process for approximately 1½ years and was fairly stable. Kerrie was the oldest of two girls. Her parents were both successful professionals. Her father was a financial planner, and her mother was an interior decorator.

Kerrie had been away from home off and on since she was 13 years old. She had her first child when she was 14½ years old. This child was privately adopted. At that time, Kerrie moved back to her parents' home and again attempted to live by her parents' rules and fit into the family. By the time she was 15½, she was again in and out of the home, and by 16 she had moved out again. This came shortly after she had been raped (an event she did not share with her parents until later in her life). Kerrie joined up with a gang and became pregnant with her second child. This time she decided to keep the baby because she thought she and the father could provide a stable environment for him. However, shortly after the baby was born, the father was incarcerated on a charge of murder and sentenced to 25 years to life.

Kerrie was devastated at this time and once again moved back into her parents' home. This is when she began attending school for a teen mothers' program. This is also when she began both individual and group therapy. Kerrie was able to address her rape issues, and during the course of this, she disclosed that she had been fondled by a next-door neighbor on several occasions while she was growing up. Kerrie often thought that if her parents had been home more often or that if they had been more emotionally involved in her life, the molestation would not have taken place. She also believed that she would have been able to share more about the rape.

The following dialogue is from the session in which Kerrie completed the letter to her "hurt child" regarding her perceived neglect by her parents. Addressing this issue in a meaningful way was very difficult for her. This was probably more difficult than the issues revolving around her molestations and the rape.

Therapist How does it feel to write your thoughts and feelings to your "hurt child?"

Kerrie It feels good, but it also makes me feel a little sad and guilty.

T Why is that, do you know?

K Yeah, on one hand I know that even if my parents had been there more for us, I still could have been molested by that guy. They probably were home some of the times it happened because I can't remember everything. And I know it wasn't their fault that I was raped. I was the one who took off from home. But yet I sometimes think that if they would have paid as much attention to us (Kerrie and her sister) as they did to their jobs, then maybe things would have been different. I don't know. . . . I just feel guilty that they worked so hard to give us everything we wanted while we were growing up and yet here I am saying they should have done more.

T Kerrie, there is a big difference between "getting all the things you want" and having the emotional support and love that you need growing up. I'm sure your parents had your best interest in mind, but there is nothing wrong with you wanting to feel important and loved.

The remainder of this session was spent discussing how Kerrie has had such a difficult time communicating her emotional needs to her "hurt child." This may be due to her belief that she does not deserve love. In addition, writing the letter allowed Kerrie to begin confronting the issue of using sex as a means of feeling close to others.

Clinical Impressions: Kerrie had internalized an image of herself as a neglected child. She was unable to articulate this for many years. Writing the letter to her "hurt child" enabled her to see this image and to confront the reality of her deep-seated feelings. Before writing the letter, Kerrie had projected the image to others that she had "perfect parents," yet she had covertly blamed them for her molestation and rape.

At this point in time, Kerrie was able to look at her family more realistically. She was able to validate her "hurt child within." The parents could then be brought into the therapy setting so that Kerrie could verbalize her feelings to them. It was obvious that the family was ready for this next step.

9

Working Through the "Stuck" Feelings

Once individuals have begun to work through the guilt and shame and have allowed themselves to address the feelings related to their losses, other feelings may begin to surface. It is important to work through these "stuck" feelings.

Many victims of child abuse may get stuck as they begin to feel anger, hurt, fear, and pain due to their inadequate coping skills. Adolescents who have been abused in early childhood may be entrenched in their concrete thinking of the world as "good" or "bad." Thus, they continue to view themselves as "good" or "bad" people rather than separating their self-worth from their feelings. This immature thinking has prevented them from emerging into healthy adolescence. They are still stuck in their earlier belief system.

As we stated in Chapter 3, it is healthy and normal to experience a variety of feelings. However, we suggest that they be viewed as "comfortable" and "safe" or as "uncomfortable," "unsafe," and "difficult" rather than as "good" or "bad." The more you can help teens accept their feelings without judgment, the easier it will be for them to recognize and work through the stuck feelings.

In addition, it is important to help adolescents understand that their experiences and the resultant feelings are separate from their sense of self-worth. "Bad" experiences do not make "bad" people. However, some teens may continue to label their abuser as "bad" and the experience as "bad." Allow the teen to do that if it helps him or her get in touch with angry feelings.

Bass and Davis (1988) aptly referred to anger as "the backbone of healing." Anger serves as an effective motivator to respond and act. Allowing oneself to feel angry counteracts the tendency to slip into feelings of hopelessness, despair, and self-blame.

Adolescents will often use anger as a defense mechanism to mask underlying feelings of fear, hurt, and pain. They tend to use anger in diffuse ways because they respond to their world in a reactive, chaotic manner, rather than focusing their energy on the underlying painful feelings that have been created by their abusers. In this respect, adolescents are not unlike their adult counterparts who have not completely worked through abuse histories and who operate from a base of anger.

If adolescents' anger is to be effective, it must be expressed appropriately and focused at people who have hurt them and who have not kept them safe. When anger is turned inward, people may become depressed, self-destructive, and filled with self-blame, which becomes self-hate. However, when individuals outwardly misdirect their anger, they tend to get out of control, and anything in their path, including themselves and others, becomes "fair game."

Teenagers who are struggling with their abuse may turn to alcohol and other drugs (AODs) as a way of coping. This is both a self-destructive act and a means of acting out their pain. It can compound the difficulties of the healing process because you are now dealing not only with the abuse history but also with the potential of addiction. If there is evidence of substance abuse, you should contact an AOD specialist.

Confronting the abuse is a necessary aspect of healing. However, confrontation does not necessarily require a direct encounter with the perpetrator(s). The necessity is to confront the underlying feelings that were created by the abuse. This may lead to direct or indirect confrontations with the individual(s) responsible for the pain and suffering the teen has incurred.

The purpose of this chapter is to help the adolescent work through stuck feelings. This includes several goals, such as identifying underlying feelings, appropriately expressing these feelings, working through anger, and confronting those responsible for the pain. Successfully completing this phase of the healing process allows the teen to achieve an integration of his or her life experiences and feelings of self-worth so that he or she can become a healthy survivor.

The activities in this chapter are designed to assist in working through feelings such as anger, hurt, and pain that often surface after the individual has worked through guilt and shame. This can be a very energized time in that the teen can become more focused and empowered in directing his or her feelings more appropriately.

As done in previous chapters, this chapter contains case studies to clarify how some of these activities have been used in actual therapy situations. We have given a brief case history, an example of dialogue during the activity, and clinical impressions.

Again, you will need to instruct the teen to read the section "Teen Talk" for Chapter 9 in the *Activity Book*. It is a good idea for you to read it also. It contains an introduction and goals for this chapter.

❏ Activity #51: Sadness

Objective: To continue processing any additional sad feelings that are still unresolved.

This activity is designed to allow adolescents to continue processing any additional sad feelings that they may still be experiencing. After teens have worked through various stages of the recovery process, they may still have feelings that are not yet resolved, or new feelings may emerge.

It is important to encourage the teen to continue the process of exploring various feelings. This activity and the next two activities are designed for this purpose. Hopefully, with this additional structured practice of "I feel" statements, the teen will incorporate this critical skill into his or her everyday life.

Ages: This activity is designed for adolescents of all ages.

Materials Needed: Activity sheet and pencil.

Instructions: Instruct the teen to think about the things that are still creating sad feelings. Once the teen has identified the specific things creating sad feelings, instruct him or her to complete the "I feel" statements. Some teens may also want to draw an accompanying picture.

Processing: After the teen has completed the activity, have him or her read the statements aloud. During processing of the statements, we have found it helpful to follow up with queries such as "Tell me about the things that are still creating sad feelings for you," "What do you want to do with your sadness?" "How do you usually express your sadness?" and "Tell me about your 'I feel' statements."

❑ **Activity #52: Fear**

Objective: To continue processing feelings that are as yet unresolved, focusing on fear.

This activity is designed to explore feelings that are still unresolved. As stated for the previous activity, many adolescents need to continue the process of exploring difficult feelings. (See Activity #51 for a more detailed explanation.)

Materials Needed: Activity sheet and pencil.

Instructions: Instruct the teen to think about the things that still make him or her feel afraid. Then have the teen complete the "I feel" statements.

Processing: After the teen has completed the activity sheet, have him or her teen read the "I feel" statements aloud. We have found it helpful to process the statements by following up with queries such as "Tell me about the things that still make you feel afraid," "What do you want to do with these scary feelings?" and "Tell me about your 'I feel' statements."

❏ Activity #53: Anger

Objective: To continue processing angry feelings that are as yet unresolved.

This activity is designed to assist the teen in processing unfinished angry feelings. (See Activity #51 for further information.)

Materials Needed: Activity sheet and pencil.

Instructions: Instruct the teen to think about the things that still make him or her feel angry. Then have him or her complete the "I feel" statements about what is still creating angry feelings.

Processing: After the teen has completed this activity, have him or her read the "I feel" statements aloud. We have found it helpful to process the statements by following up with queries such as "Tell me about the things that still make you feel angry," "What do you want to do with your angry feelings?" "How do you normally take care of your angry feelings?" and "Tell me about your 'I feel' statements."

❏ Activity #54: Tanya's Story

Objective: To explore some of the healthy and unhealthy ways to express anger through the medium of storytelling.

This activity is designed to introduce and explore some of the healthy and unhealthy ways that individuals express anger. It is common for many abused teens to harbor unresolved feelings that manifest themselves as anger and rage. These adolescents typically need to develop and practice healthy skills and to express feelings.

The story of Tanya explores how one teen was able to move from unhealthy expressions of anger to healthier means of expressing herself without hurting others. Many of the behaviors mentioned in this story are common to abused teens.

Ages: This activity is designed for adolescents of all ages.

Materials Needed: Activity sheet, pencil, and crayons, colored pencils, and/or markers.

Instructions: Instruct the teen to read the story of Tanya and complete the related questions. Then have him or her draw a picture of Tanya.

Note: The academically challenged teen may need you to read the story to him or her.

Processing: After the teen is finished reading the story and has completed the questions, have him or her read the answers aloud. While processing the story, we have found it helpful to ask questions such as "What do you think about the story?" "How did Tanya feel in the story? Why?" and "Have you ever felt like Tanya? What did you do?"

Ask the teen to share his or her drawing of Tanya. It may be informative for you to note whether Tanya is drawn acting out her anger or dealing with it in a healthy way.

Case Example: *Denise*

Brief Case History: Denise was a 16-year-old African American girl who had been placed in a residential treatment center following a stay in an acute unit of a psychiatric hospital. Denise had taken a knife and slashed her wrists in front of her parents while they were fighting one night. Before this suicidal gesture, Denise had acted out her anger by running away, destroying furniture, and slapping her mother. Her mother was now afraid of her and refused to let her come home for visits until she was sure Denise had control of her temper. The mother told the therapist during the intake session that she believed that Denise had been molested around the age of 6 by her first husband's brother, but she was vague in saying why she had reached that conclusion. Denise's mother was sure that was why Denise was so mad all the time.

Denise was a bright, very talkative person. She got irritated rather quickly, but just as quickly would catch herself and calm down. She wondered why she was not getting as mad in her placement as she did at home. Denise had been in treatment for approximately 2 months when she did the above activity in group. The following dialogue took place.

Therapist What were the unhealthy ways Tanya took care of her anger?

Denise She would slam doors and throw things. She didn't care if anybody got hurt. I used to be that way, but I don't want to do that stuff anymore. . . . I don't feel like it anymore. . . . I wish I could go home so I could show my parents that I've changed.

T Speaking of parents, what did Tanya learn from her parents about anger?

D Let me say! Let me say! (Insisting on answering first). The father used to hit his wife, and that made Tanya think it was okay!

T What else happened as a result of the father hitting the mother?

Peer Then the mother hit Tanya, and Tanya probably hit the dog! (group laughter)

T You have a point there. When someone just absorbs the hurt and anger, sometimes they transfer it to someone else. And what if that someone else doesn't understand what's going on or can't protect themselves?

D I know, I know! Then Tanya thought it was her fault, she thought she deserved it, and then she thought she could get away with being mean to everybody else! You know, when my parents were fighting that night when they took me to the hospital, I was so sick of them yelling and hitting each other all the time. They never paid any attention to me, except to be mad at me when I did something bad, but I didn't care. . . . How could they tell me not to do mean things when they were always being mean to me and my sister? I thought maybe I could make them see how mean they were when I grabbed that knife, but they didn't even notice until I put my bloody arm right in their face!

The group session continued to process feelings regarding "Tanya's Story."

Clinical Impressions: Denise was acting out legitimate anger in her home environment. However, her models for the expression of anger were unhealthy ones. Her mother's denial of the violent relationship between her and her husband only made things harder for Denise. Denise was the classic scapegoat for the family's problems. It was easier for the parents to make Denise the problem than to deal with their own issues. In a different environment, Denise was amazed that she was not angry and upset all the time and that when she was, she could control herself. She had gotten so used to being told what a "bad" child she was that she could hardly believe that staff and peers liked her irrepressible personality. This gave Denise the opportunity to create a new self-image and to look at her family situation for what it was. This made her angry all over again, for she realized she could have wound up killing herself in an effort to gain her parents' love.

Once Denise had processed the above realization, she was able to participate in plans to live with her grandmother after discharge. She was very worried about her mother and sister, but she felt helpless to change the situation. She visited her sister as much as possible when the father was away and planned on having her sister live with her when she was older.

❑ **Activity #55: My Contract**

Objective: To develop a plan to appropriately express and work through difficult feelings.

This activity is designed to assist the teen in developing a plan to appropriately express and work through difficult feelings. The use of contracting is one way of empowering the teen to develop a plan of action for future times when he or she feels "stuck."

Contracting is not a new phenomenon. This therapeutic tool has been found to be extremely useful in promoting change. When an individual makes a promise to him- or herself, as well as to the therapist, this can be a pivotal point in the healing process. The contract is individually designed to meet the unique needs of the adolescent creating the contract.

In addition, we have found in our experience that writing the contract in the teen's own handwriting makes it more binding. When an individual is in the midst of his or her stuck feelings, it can be a powerful experience to read his or her own personal commitment made in a less emotionally chaotic time.

Ages: Adolescents of all ages should have no problem coming up with ways to express themselves, such as writing, drawing, talking to someone, or doing a physical activity.

Materials Needed: Activity sheet and pencil.

Instructions: Instruct the teen to think about the different ways of expressing feelings that have been explored in previous activities. Then have him or her identify specific ways that will best help in the expression of angry, hurt, or sad feelings.

Once the adolescent has identified the best ways for him or her to take care of difficult feelings, use the activity form to write these ideas into a contract.

Processing: After the teen has completed the contract, have him or her read it aloud. While processing the contract, we have found it helpful to follow up with queries such as "Tell me about your contract," "What do you think might get in the way of doing some of these things? Why?" and "What things do you think will be the most helpful? Why?"

❏ Activity #56: Beginning My Journal

Objective: To learn how to record thoughts and feelings in a journal.

This activity is designed to help the adolescent develop a tool that can assist him or her on a lifelong journey as a survivor. Writing thoughts and feelings in a journal can be extremely insightful and therapeutic. Writing down feelings can really help with obsessional thoughts that continue to haunt the individual. This serves to move the thoughts and feelings from the head to the paper, which makes them more tangible and easier to handle.

It is important for you as the therapist to realize that this is just the beginning of learning the process of journal writing. For the teen to utilize this tool, he or she will need to be encouraged to practice this exercise outside the therapy sessions. Once the teen really learns this tool, it can be invaluable.

Ages: This activity is designed for adolescents of all ages.

Materials Needed: Activity sheet and pencil.

Instructions: Instruct the teen to write down his or her feelings for that day. Encourage the teen to express why he or she is having the particular feelings. Also, you might want to encourage the teen to write any additional thoughts he or she is having.

Processing: After the teen has completed this activity, have him or her read the journal entry aloud. While processing this activity, we have found it helpful to follow up with queries such as "Tell me about your journal entry," "How did you feel while writing about your feelings today?" "How do you think writing about your feelings can help you? Why?" and "Is there anything else you want to add to your journal?"

❑ Activity #57: You Hurt Me!

Objective: To express feelings in the form of a letter.

This activity is designed to enable the teen to express his or her feelings toward the abuser in a direct but less threatening way. Writing a therapeutic letter allows the individual to focus feelings appropriately at those who have hurt him or her.

As stated in the introduction to this chapter, when anger is turned inward, adolescents may become depressed, self-destructive, and filled with self-blame, which may become self-hate. Equally danger-ous is misdirected anger, which can get out of control. Confronting the abuser is a necessary aspect of healing, but it does not need to be done with a direct encounter with the abuser. Writing a therapeu-tic letter has been found to be a powerful technique in this process.

Ages: This activity is designed for adolescents of all ages.

Note: This activity may elicit a variety of feelings. As the therapist, you will want to be acutely aware of the teen's feelings and reactions so that you can assist in processing feelings.

Materials Needed: Activity sheet and pencils.

Instructions: Instruct the teen to think about the things he or she would like to be able to say to the person(s) who hurt him or her. Then have the teen write a letter to the person(s) who was/were abusive. Encourage the teen to include specifics regarding what the person(s) did, how the teen felt then and now, and what the teen would like to be able to do with the feelings.

Note: It is not uncommon for people to become very graphic in their descriptions of what they would like to do to the person(s). It is important to allow the teen to express and fully process his or her thoughts and feelings.

Processing: After the teen has completed his or her letter, it is impor-tant to process the letter by following up with queries such as "Tell me about your letter," "How did it feel to write the letter? Why?" "How does it feel to express your feelings to the person(s) who hurt you? Why?" and "Is there anything else you would like to add to your letter?"

Case Example: *Valerie*

Brief Case History: Valerie was a 15-year-old Caucasian teen who was under the guardianship of Child Protective Services (CPS). Because of extensive self-harming behavior (scratching and cutting on herself) and two suicide gestures, Valerie was placed in residential treatment. Valerie had been physically and emotionally abused by her biological father and then had been molested by her stepbrother for 2 years. Valerie's mother had been molested herself as a young teenager and had never discussed this with anyone until she brought it up in Valerie's family therapy. The stepbrother was vaguely apologetic about the molestation, mostly complaining about how much he had suffered having to go to court. The mother was angry at Valerie for "breaking up" the family, although at this point Valerie was the only one out of the home. The mother also blamed Valerie for revealing the abuse, accusing her of doing it to get "attention." In the face of these accusations, Valerie would become quite defensive, attempting to placate her mother. She also tried to let the stepbrother off the hook by acknowledging that he "had problems too."

Soon after these sessions and after conflictual phone conversations with her mother, Valerie would tell staff that she felt like hurting herself. As a result, family therapy was put on hold, and phone contact was supervised. Valerie was asked to complete the above activity for an individual therapy session. When she brought a 10-page letter to the session, she asked if she could read it aloud. After doing so, the following dialogue took place.

Therapist Valerie, that was quite a letter! You expressed a lot of hurt and anger toward your mother. What was it like to write it?

Valerie At first I had to kind of force myself to write it, but then I started to get into it. I don't know—now I feel guilty reading it to you.

T Are you doing something wrong by expressing these feelings?

V I've never told my mother how I really felt. She always gets so upset and she never really listens to me, so what's the point?

T The point is just that by writing the letter you get to say how you really feel without worrying about your mother's reaction. You can say whatever you like about your hurt.

V That's true, but I feel guilty even if she never reads this.

T How do you usually feel around your mother?

V Like I have to be really careful about what I say. She blames me for everything.

T   So this guilty feeling is something you carry around with you?
V   Yeah, I guess that's true, I do feel that way a lot, even here in treatment.
T   I thought it was interesting that you chose to write to your mother and not your stepbrother.
V   That's weird—I didn't even think of him when you asked me to write this.

Clinical Impressions: Valerie was an intelligent, insightful adolescent who was very unsure of herself. Her mother's constant doubting and criticism of her had taken its toll. Valerie was angry at her mother not only because the mother had failed to protect her from being abused by two men in the family but particularly because her mother did not listen to her or try to understand her. Valerie felt betrayed by her mother.

As her therapy continued, it became clear that Valerie's self-harming and suicidal gestures had been a cry for help directed at the mother. The self-harm also was an expression of self-destructive anger. When these actions brought no response other than more anger, Valerie felt extraordinarily helpless. Progressing through the activities in the *Activity Book* as well as having supportive, therapeutic relationships with both male and female staff aided Valerie in becoming more self-affirming. It was very difficult for Valerie to become more detached emotionally from her mother, but she did begin to understand the necessity of this. It was also important for Valerie to focus on the hurt she had experienced from her father and her stepbrother, to whom she eventually wrote unsent letters as well. Valerie's mother was strongly urged to attend her own therapy to work on healing her past. The stepbrother was sentenced to 6 months in jail and 2 years' probation with counseling after a plea of a lesser charge.

PHASE IV

Becoming Future Oriented

10

What Have I Learned?

When the adolescent reaches this point, he or she has attained many goals in the healing process and should be at a fairly stable point in his or her recovery. Therefore, the overwhelming feelings of victimization have subsided, allowing the teen to focus on present living versus past experiences. Now the task becomes learning the skills to move forward successfully.

It is important to point out that the healing process cannot be rushed. There are no clear definitions of beginning and ending points. Some people will need to repeat all or some of the prior stages before they can resolve their early traumas.

The purpose of this chapter is to have the adolescent assess what he or she has learned about the abuse and to identify the new skills that he or she has acquired in completing these activities. Once the teen has integrated the new learning into day-to-day living, he or she will feel more balanced. There will be movement from feelings of fragmentation to a sense of wholeness.

The activities in this chapter are designed to assist in reviewing the many goals that have been attained during the healing process.

In assisting the teen with the activities in this chapter, you may gain some insight as to whether it is necessary to repeat any of the activities from the previous chapters. If it seems as though the teen is still struggling with particular issues, you may decide to repeat some of the previous activities particular to his or her needs.

As in previous chapters, we have included case studies to assist you in further understanding of how some of the activities have been used in actual therapy situations. We have given a brief case history, an example of dialogue, and clinical impressions.

You will need to instruct the adolescent to read the section "Teen Talk" for this chapter in the *Activity Book*. You will find it helpful to read it also so that you both are aware of the goals for this chapter.

We hope that this book has been helpful in your work with abused adolescents.

❏ **Activity #58: Pride List**

Objective: To identify therapeutic accomplishments.

This activity is designed to encourage the teen to identify his or her therapeutic accomplishments. Abusive experiences can be so damaging to self-esteem that it can be difficult for individuals to acknowledge their progress toward a healthier, more integrated sense of self. Because abused teens are often stuck in their abusive experiences, a review of their progress will assist them in focusing on positive changes and personal growth.

Ages: This activity is designed for adolescents of all ages.

Materials Needed: Activity sheet, pencil.

Instructions: Instruct the teen to think about all the hard work he or she has done so far. Ask him or her to think about all the new things that he or she has learned that make him or her feel proud. Then have the teen list what things make him or her feel proud.

Processing: After the teen has completed his or her Pride List, it is important to have the teen read it aloud. We have found it helpful to follow up with queries such as "Tell me about the things that make you feel proud," "Which one of the things you listed are you most proud of? Why?" and "Of the new things you have learned, which one do you think is the most important? Why?"

❏ **Activity #59: Self-Affirmations**

Objective: To be able to list positive self-attributes.

This activity is designed to assist the teen in describing the things learned that he or she listed in Activity #58 as skills or attributes that can now be found within him- or herself. It is important to assist the teen in this integration process so that these skills or attributes can become part of the adolescent's "core." Hopefully, this will assist in the process of strengthening the teen's sense of self.

Ages: Adolescents of all ages should be able to complete this activity.

Materials Needed: Activity sheet, pencil.

Instructions: Instruct the adolescent to think about all the new things that have been learned and how they make him or her feel. Then ask the teen to think about what things make him or her feel special. Explain that the statements about the special things can also be referred to as "self-affirmations." Next, have the teen list or write about these self-affirmations.

Processing: After the teen has completed this activity, have him or her read it aloud. While processing this activity, we have found it helpful to follow up with queries such as "Tell me about the things you like about yourself," "What things make you feel special?" "Of the things you listed, which one do you like the most? Why?" and "Is there anything else you want to add to your list? What?"

❑ **Activity #60: Things I've Learned**

Objective: To identify what has been learned.
  This activity is designed to assist the teen in exploring and organizing what has been learned after completing the activities in this book.

Ages: Adolescents of all ages are capable of identifying and writing about what has been learned.

Instructions: Instruct the teen to think about what he or she feels are the most important things that he or she has learned after finishing the activities in this book. Then have him or her write about them.

Materials Needed: Activity sheet and pencil.

Processing: After the teen has completed this activity, have him or her read the essay aloud. While processing, we have found it helpful to follow up with queries such as "Tell me about the things you have learned," "Which one of these things do you think is the most important? Why?" "Which one of these things do you think will be the most helpful to you? Why?" and "Would you like to add anything else to your list?"

Case Example: *Sonya*

Brief Case History: Sonya was a 15-year-old Caucasian girl who had been adopted when she was 4 years old. She knew nothing about her biological parents and felt frustrated because she could not remember them at all. Sonya had been in placement in a residential treatment facility for about 18 months. Her parents had not attended one family therapy session during this time, much to the consternation of the adoption services agency that was paying for Sonya's treatment, as well of the facility staff.
  When Sonya was admitted to the facility, she looked like a scared rabbit; she was disheveled, had poor hygiene, and was actively dissociating. She had been found wandering the streets of the Las Vegas strip at 3 a.m. Her arms had scars as well as fresh scratches on them. After a stay in an acute unit to stabilize her, Sonya was

transferred to the residential facility. Because Sonya had been molested at age 11 by a 19-year-old male, she was referred to the facility's group for traumatized adolescents. However, it soon became clear that Sonya could not function in the group in that she continued to severely dissociate. It was decided that her individual therapist would work with her in a supportive manner until Sonya became more able to invest actively in her treatment.

After approximately 6 months, Sonya approached the group therapist, asking to return to group. She appeared much brighter in both affect and mood and after consultation with the treatment team, she again became part of group. Sonya worked hard in group for the next year, with many ups and downs. Although she no longer dissociated, she sometimes had a "spacy" look in her eyes when she was uncomfortable. Sonya had not understood what "listening to oneself" meant; her only reality was the one defined for her by others—her parents (who, though absent, seemed to control her) and the 19-year-old molester whom she had thought of as her "boyfriend." Sonya was afraid of her feelings and thoughts. When she felt good, she was scared and felt tempted to harm herself. At times she impulsively acted out in a sexual manner and then was racked by guilt over how "bad" she was. Sonya kept a journal for the first time, talked a lot in group, and learned to go to staff with problems. She was not very discerning in whom she chose to talk with at times and then felt embarrassed at the reaction she got.

Sonya had worked her way through most of the activities in her *Activity Book*. After she completed the essay about what she had learned, Sonya hesitatingly read it aloud to her peers.

Therapist That's quite a list of things, Sonya! You must be very proud!

Sonya I guess. . . . I feel funny saying all these things about myself.

Peer You know you did all those things!

S I know, but it's such a struggle for me to accept it. . . . In spite of everything, there's still a part of me that says it can't be true—that what my parents think of me is right.

T So, how can you deal with that?

S Just tell myself that's my old way of seeing myself and it's not really true. I know it's not true. . . . I know that Jason really molested me and that it wasn't my fault. He made me feel special and I needed that. I still need it, but I have to find it in better ways.

T   So what was the most important thing you learned?

S   That I can make myself feel special and loved by paying attention to that feeling inside that tells me what's going on. That I can stay safe.

T   That's great, Sonya, congratulations!

Clinical Impressions: Sonya came to treatment at a critical stage. She had seemed headed toward suicide if there had been no intervention. On the Trauma Symptom Checklist for Children (TSCC; Briere, 1996) administered to Sonya after admission, Sonya scored quite high on the Dissociation subscale. Although she had once needed to use this defense as a coping skill, it was not helping her in her treatment. Eventually Sonya felt safe enough to use her ability to dissociate only occasionally. She required the security and safety of developing a therapeutic relationship with her individual therapist before she could open up in group. Once she was able to work actively in group, she worked very hard to learn to listen to herself. She began to recognize that she had an "inner voice" that could tell her what she was feeling and what was going on in her environment.

As Sonya continued to struggle with this concept, she began to incorporate and internalize healthy coping skills. She became more assertive with her peers and adults. She was able to recover quickly from negative phone conversations with her parents. She read aloud in group therapeutic letters to both her biological and adoptive parents. Although Sonya had intellectually accepted that the sexual relationship was unhealthy and inappropriate, she did not view it solely as a molestation; part of her still held on to the mistaken belief that she had been "loved." This indicates that Sonya still has work to do in this area in her individual outpatient therapy.

❑ **Activity #61: Self-Portrait**

Objective: To draw a picture of oneself as seen after completing activities in this book.

This activity is designed to help you assess how the teen now sees him- or herself. This activity can also be beneficial in revealing to the teen his or her own growth. You can facilitate this process by having the teen compare this activity to the self-portrait he or she did in Activity #2 in Chapter 2.

Ages: Adolescents of all ages should be able to complete this activity unassisted.

Materials Needed: Activity sheet and pencils, crayons, markers, and/ or colored pencils.

Instructions: Instruct the teen to draw a picture of how he or she sees him- or herself today. Encourage the teen to be as complete as possible.

Note: The more mature teen will be more detailed in his or her drawing. However, there will most likely be a change from the first self-portrait to the second regardless of the teen's age or functioning level.

Processing: After the teen has completed the drawing, it is important to discuss it by following up with queries such as "Tell me about your drawing," "Tell me how you feel in this picture. Why?" and "How is this picture different from the picture you drew in Activity #2 in the second chapter? Why?"

Appendix: Child Abuse Trauma Interview for Adolescents (CATI-AD)

NAME: _____ DATE:_____

DOB:_____ CHRONOLOGICAL AGE:_____

PRIMARY THERAPIST: _____

INTERVIEWER:_____ DATE OF INTERVIEW:_____

BACKGROUND INFORMATION

1. Biological parents' marital status _____
   Number of marriages _____
2. Who do you live with? _____ If not with parents,
   why? _____
   _____
3. List siblings, including ages: _____
   _____

4. Did you ever live out of your home? _____ If yes, with whom?

_____

_____

5. Were you ever in juvenile detention? _____ If yes, describe:

_____

_____

6. Have you ever used alcohol or other drugs (AODs)? _____
   Describe: _____

_____

7. Have either of your parents had problems with alcohol or other
   drugs (AODs)? yes _____ no _____
   If yes, what? _____

_____

8. Did the AODs cause any problems? _____ If so, what?_____

_____

_____

9. Did you ever see one parent (or step-parent) hit or beat up the
   other parent or a sibling? yes _____ no _____
   If yes, describe what happened: _____

_____

10. Were either of your parents sexually or physically abused as a
    child? _____ If yes, describe: _____

_____

11. Have you experienced any significant losses/deaths in the last 2
    years (friends/family)? _____ Who? _____

_____

PSYCHOLOGICAL/EMOTIONAL MALTREATMENT

Have you ever experienced any of the following? If so, how often?

	Never 0	Some- times 1	Lots of Times 2	Most of the Time 3
1. _____ Being yelled at	0	1	2	3
2. _____ Insulted	0	1	2	3
3. _____ Criticized	0	1	2	3

4. ___ Made to feel guilty	0	1	2	3
5. ___ Ridiculed or humiliated	0	1	2	3
6. ___ Embarrassed in front of others	0	1	2	3
7. ___ Made to feel that you were a bad person	0	1	2	3
8. ___ Given "Silent treatment"	0	1	2	3
9. ___ Locked in a room, closet, or other small place	0	1	2	3
10. ___ Tied to something	0	1	2	3
11. ___ Threatened to harm you	0	1	2	3
12. ___ Threatened to harm someone you care about	0	1	2	3
13. ___ Threatened to harm your pet	0	1	2	3
14. ___ Threatened to leave you somewhere	0	1	2	3
15. ___ Threatened to leave and never come back	0	1	2	3
16. ___ Other: _____	0	1	2	3

PHYSICAL MALTREATMENT

Have you ever experienced any of the following? If so, how often?

	Never 0	Some- times 1	Lots of Times 2	Most of the Time 3
1. ___ Spanked	0	1	2	3
2. ___ Hit/slapped	0	1	2	3
3. ___ Punched	0	1	2	3
4. ___ Pulled hair	0	1	2	3

5.	____ Scratched	0	1	2	3
6.	____ Twisted arm	0	1	2	3
7.	____ Pushed	0	1	2	3
8.	____ Banged head	0	1	2	3
9.	____ Attempted drowning	0	1	2	3
10.	____ Broken bones or teeth	0	1	2	3
11.	____ Cuts or bruises	0	1	2	3
12.	____ Other:_____	0	1	2	3

13. Was CPS or the police ever notified? ___ yes ___ no
    If yes, what happened

    _____

    _____

14. Did you ever need medical treatment for your injuries? _____
    If yes, describe: _____

    _____

SEXUAL MALTREATMENT

1. Age of first sexual experience: _____
   Describe: _____

   _____

   _____

2. Has anyone ever kissed you in a way that made you feel uncomfortable? ____ yes _____ no
   If yes, indicate who: _____

   _____

   Describe what happened: _____

   _____

3. Have you ever seen or been made to view sexually explicit videos,
   magazines, pictures, etc.? _____ If yes, describe: _____

   _____

   _____

4. Has anyone ever exposed him/herself to you in a sexual way or
   made you undress in front of him/her? _____
   If yes, indicate who: _____
   Describe what happened: _____

   _____

5. Has anyone ever touched your body in a way that made you feel uncomfortable? _____ If yes, indicate who: _____

Describe what happened: _____

6. Has anyone ever made you touch them in a way that made you feel uncomfortable? _____ yes _____ no
If yes, indicate who: _____
Describe what happened: _____

7. Has anyone ever put anything in your private parts or made you have oral sex with them? _____
If yes, indicate who: _____
Describe what happened: _____

8. Have you ever touched anyone sexually who was 4 or more years younger than you? _____ If yes, describe (include ages): _____

9. Was CPS or the police ever notified concerning any of the above questions? _____ If yes, describe (include dates or age at time):

ADDITIONAL INFORMATION

Additional information regarding psychological/emotional, physical, or sexual maltreatment:

_____

_____

_____

_____

_____

_____

_____

_____

_____

SIGNATURE   DATE

References

Achenbach, T. M. (1991). *Manual for the child behavior checklist: 1991 profile*. Burlington, VT: University of Vermont, Department of Psychiatry.

American Professional Society on the Abuse of Children. (1990). *Guidelines for psychosocial evaluation of suspected sexual abuse of young children*. Chicago: Author.

American Professional Society on the Abuse of Children. (1992). *Advisor, 5*(3), 1-25.

American Professional Society on the Abuse of Children. (1995). *Psychosocial evaluation of suspected psychological maltreatment in children and adolescents: Practice guidelines*. Chicago: Author.

American Psychiatric Association. (1968). *Diagnostic and statistical manual of mental disorders* (2nd ed.). Washington, DC: Author.

American Psychiatric Association. (1980). *Diagnostic and statistical manual of mental disorders* (3rd ed.). Washington, DC: Author.

American Psychiatric Association. (1987). *Diagnostic and statistical manual of mental disorders* (3rd ed., Rev.). Washington, DC: Author.

American Psychiatric Association. (1994). *Diagnostic and statistical manual of mental disorders* (4th ed.). Washington, DC: Author.

Barbaree, H. E., Marshall, W. L., & Hudson, S. M. (Eds.). (1993). *The juvenile sex offender*. New York: Guilford.

Bass, E., & Davis, L. (1988). *The courage to heal: A guide for women survivors of child sexual abuse*. New York: Perennial.

Beck, A. T., & Emery, G. (1985). *Anxiety disorders and phobias: A cognitive perspective*. New York: Basic Books.

Bergstrom, S., & Cruz, L. (1980). *Lesbian and gay male sexuality and lifestyles: A teacher's source book*. San Francisco: Human Rights Foundation.

Bergstrom, S., & Cruz, L. (Eds.). (1983). *Counseling lesbian and gay youth*. Washington, DC: National Network of Runaway and Youth Services.

Berliner, L., & Conte, J. (1995). The effects of disclosure and intervention on sexually abused children. *Child Abuse and Neglect, 19*, 371-384.

Berman, P. (1994). *Therapeutic exercises for victimized and neglected girls: Applications for individual, family, and group psychotherapy*. Sarasota, FL: Professional Resource Press.

Bolton, F., & Bolton, S. (1987). *Working with violent families*. Newbury Park, CA: Sage.

Bolton, F., Morris, L., & MacEachron, A. (1989). *Males at risk: The other side of child sexual abuse*. Thousand Oaks, CA: Sage.

Briere, J. (1989). *Therapy for adults molested as children: Beyond survival*. New York: Springer.

Briere, J. (1992). *Child abuse trauma: Theory and treatment of the lasting effects*. Newbury Park, CA: Sage.

Briere, J. (1996). *Trauma symptom checklist for children (TSCC): Professional manual*. Odessa, FL: Psychological Assessment Resources.

Briere, J., & Conte, J. (1993). Self-reported amnesia for abuse in adults molested as children. *Journal of Traumatic Stress, 6*(1), 21-31.

Briere, J., & Runtz, M. (1989). The Trauma Symptom Checklist (TSC-33): Early data on a new scale. *Journal of Interpersonal Violence, 4*, 151-163.

Bukowski, W. M., Sippola, L., & Brender, W. (1993). Where does sexuality come from? Normative sexuality from a developmental perspective. In H. E. Barbaree, W. L. Marshall, & S. M. Hudson (Eds.), *The juvenile sex offender* (pp. 84-103). New York: Guilford.

Burgess, A. W., & Holmstrom, L. (1978). Accessory-to-sex: Pressure, sex, and secrecy. In A. W. Burgess, A. Groth, L. Holmstrom, & S. Sgroi (Eds.), *Sexual assault of children and adolescents*. Lexington, MA: Lexington.

Burns, D. D. (1989). *The feeling good handbook*. New York: Plume.

Cantlay, L. (1996). *Detecting child abuse: Recognizing children at risk through drawings*. Santa Barbara, CA: Holly.

Conte, J., Briere, J., & Sexton, D. (1989, August). *Moderators of the long-term effects of sexual abuse*. Paper presented at the annual meeting of the American Psychological Association, New Orleans.

Coulborn-Faller, K., & Corwin, D. (1995). Children's interview statements and behaviors: Roles in identifying sexually abused children. *Child Abuse and Neglect, 19*, 71-82.

Coulborn-Faller, K., & Everson, M. (Eds.). (1996a). Child interviewing, Part I. *Child Maltreatment, 1*(3).

Coulborn-Faller, K., & Everson, M. (Eds.). (1996b). Child interviewing, Part II. *Child Maltreatment, 1*(4).

Courtois, C. A. (1988). *Healing the incest wound: Adult survivors in therapy*. New York: Norton.

Crowder, A. (1995). *Opening the door: A treatment model for therapy with male survivors of sexual abuse*. New York: Brunner/Mazel.

Crowley, R. J., & Mills, J. C. (1989). *Cartoon magic*. New York: Brunner/Mazel.

Cunningham, C., & MacFarlane, K. (1991). *When children molest children: Group treatment strategies for young sexual abusers*. Orwell, VT: Safer Society.

Doris, J. (Ed.). (1991). *The suggestibility of children's recollections*. Washington, DC: American Psychological Association.

Dutton, D. G. (1995). *The batterer: A psychological profile.* New York: Basic Books.

Dutton, D. G., & Painter, S. (1981). Traumatic bonding: The development of emotional attachment in battered women and other relationships of intermittent abuse. *Journal of Victimology, 6,* 139-155.

Elliott, D. M., & Briere, J. (1992). Sexual abuse trauma among professional women: Validating the trauma symptom checklist-40 (TSC-40). *Child Abuse and Neglect, 16,* 391-398.

Elson, M. (1987). *The Kohut seminars on self psychology and psychotherapy with adolescents and young adults.* New York: Norton.

Everstine, D. S., & Everstine, L. (1989). *Sexual trauma in children and adolescents.* New York: Brunner/Mazel.

Everstine, D. S., & Everstine, L. (1993). *The trauma response: Treatment for emotional injury.* New York: Norton.

Ewing, C. P. (1987). *Battered women who kill.* Lexington, MA: Lexington.

Finkelhor, D. (1984). *Child sexual abuse: New theory and research.* New York: Free Press.

Finkelhor, D., with Araji, S., Baron, L., Browne, A., Peters, S. D., & Wyatt, G. E. (1986). *A sourcebook on child sexual abuse.* Newbury Park, CA: Sage.

Finkelhor, D., & Browne, A. (1986). Initial and long-term effects: A conceptual framework. In D. Finkelhor (with S. Araji, L. Baron, A. Browne, S. D. Peters, & G. E. Wyatt), *A sourcebook on child sexual abuse.* Newbury Park, CA: Sage.

Finkelhor, D., Hotaling, G., Lewis, I. A., & Smith, C. (1989). Sexual abuse and its relationship to later sexual satisfaction, marital status, religion, and attitudes. *Journal of Interpersonal Violence, 4,* 279-399.

Freud, S. (1986). The aetiology of hysteria. In S. Strachey & A. Freud (Eds.), *The standard edition of the complete psychological works of Sigmund Freud.* London: Hogarth.

Friedrich, W. N. (1990). Developmental considerations. In W. N. Friedrich, *Psychotherapy of sexually abused children and their families.* New York: Norton.

Friedrich, W. N. (Ed.). (1991). *Casebook of sexual abuse treatment.* New York: Norton.

Friedrich, W. N. (1995). *Psychotherapy with sexually abused boys: An integrated approach.* Thousand Oaks, CA: Sage.

Fromuth, M. E. (1986). The relationship of childhood sexual abuse with later psychological and sexual adjustment in a sample of college women. *Child Abuse and Neglect, 10,* 5-16.

Garbarino, J., Guttmann, E., & Seeley, J. (1986). *The psychologically battered child: Strategies for identification, assessment and intervention.* San Francisco: Jossey-Bass.

Gil, E. (1991). *The healing power of play: Therapy with abused children.* New York: Guilford.

Gil, E. (1992, October). *Treatment of abused and sexualized children.* Workshop presented in Boise, ID.

Gil, E. (1996). *Treating abused adolescents.* New York: Guilford Press.

Gil, E., & Johnson, T. C. (1993). *Sexualized children: Assessment and treatment of sexualized children and children who molest.* Rockville, MD: Launch.

Goodman, M. S., & Fallon, B. C. (1995). *Pattern changing for abused women: An educational program.* [Suppl.]. Thousand Oaks, CA: Sage.

Haugaard, J. J., & Reppucci, N. D. (1988). *The sexual abuse of children.* San Francisco: Jossey-Bass.

Helfer, R. E. (1987). The developmental basis of child abuse and neglect: An epidemiological approach. In R. E. Helfer & R. S. Kempe (Eds.), *The battered child* (4th ed.). Chicago: University of Chicago Press.

Helfer, R. E., & Kempe, R. S. (Eds.). (1987). *The battered child* (4th ed.). Chicago: University of Chicago Press.

Henschel, D., Briere, J., Magallanes, M., & Smiljanich, K. (1990, April). *Sexual abuse related attributions: Probing the role of "traumagenic factors."* Paper presented at the annual meeting of the Western Psychological Association, Los Angeles.

Hepworth, D. H., & Larsen, J. (1993). *Direct social work practice: Theory and skills.* Belmont, CA: Brooks/Cole.

Herman, J. (1981). *Father-daughter incest.* Cambridge, MA: Harvard University Press.

Herman, J. (1992). *Trauma and recovery: The aftermath of violence—from domestic abuse to political terror.* New York: Basic Books.

Hunter, M. (1989). *Abused boys: The neglected victims of sexual abuse.* Lexington, MA: Lexington.

Karp, C. L. (1995). The repressed memory controversy. *Family Advocate, 11*(3), 70-71, 85.

Karp, C. L. (1996, September). *Talking to children: Clinical vs. forensic interviews.* Paper presented at the fourth annual conference of the Arizona Professional Society on the Abuse of Children, Tucson.

Karp, C. L., & Butler, T. L. (1996). *Treatment strategies for abused children: From victim to survivor.* Thousand Oaks, CA: Sage.

Karp, L., & Karp, C. L. (1989, with Suppl. 1996). *Domestic torts: Family violence, conflict and sexual abuse.* New York: Clark Boardman Callaghan.

Kaufman, B., & Wohl, A. (1992). *Casualties of childhood: A developmental perspective on sexual abuse using projective drawings.* New York: Brunner/Mazel.

Kinsey, A., Pomeroy, W. B., & Martin, C. E. (1948). *Sexual behavior in the human male.* Philadelphia: W. B. Saunders.

Kinsey, A., Pomeroy, W. B., Martin, C. E., & Gebhard, P. H. (1953). *Sexual behavior in the human female.* Philadelphia: W. B. Saunders.

Kohut, H. (1977). *The restoration of the self.* Madison, CT: International Universities Press.

Kohut, H. (1971). *The analysis of the self.* New York: International Universities Press.

Kroll, J. (1993). *PTSD/borderlines in therapy: Finding the balance.* New York: Norton.

MacFarlane, K., & Waterman, J. (1986). *Sexual abuse of young children.* New York: Guilford.

Malchiodi, C. (1990). *Breaking the silence: Art therapy with children from violent homes.* New York: Brunner/Mazel.

Martinson, F. M. (1991). Normal sexual development in infancy and childhood. In G. D. Ryan & S. L. Lane (Eds.), *Juvenile sexual offending.* New York: Lexington.

Mills, J. C., & Crowley, R. J. (1986). *Therapeutic metaphors for children and the child within.* New York: Brunner/Mazel.

Morris, L. A. (1997). *The male heterosexual.* Thousand Oaks, CA: Sage.

National Adolescent Perpetrator Network. (1988). Preliminary report from the National Task Force on Juvenile Sexual Offending 1988. *Juvenile and Family Court Journal, 39*(2).

Pearlman, L., & Saakvitne, K. (1995). *Trauma and the therapist: Countertransference and vicarious traumatization in psychotherapy with incest survivors.* New York: Norton.

Peters, S. D. (1988). Child sexual abuse and later psychological problems. In G. E. Wyatt & G. J. Powell (Eds.), *Lasting effects of child sexual abuse* (pp. 108-118). Newbury Park, CA: Sage.

Roche, E. (1983). Residential care for gay and lesbian adolescents. In S. Bergstrom & L. Cruz (Eds.), *Counseling lesbian and gay youth.* Washington, DC: National Network of Runaway and Youth Services.

Rutter, M. (1971). Normal sexual development. *Journal of Child Psychology and Psychiatry, 11*, 259-283.

Sgroi, S. M. (1982). *Handbook of clinical intervention in child sexual abuse.* Lexington, MA: Lexington.

Sgroi, S. M. (1988). *Vulnerable populations* (Vol. 1). Lexington, MA: Lexington.

Sidun, N. M., & Rosenthal, R. H. (1987). Graphic indicators of sexual abuse in Draw-A-Person tests of psychiatrically hospitalized adolescents. *The Arts in Psychotherapy, 14*, 25-33.

Simonds, S. (1994). *Bridging the silence: Nonverbal modalities in the treatment of adult survivors of childhood sexual abuse.* New York: Norton.

Stern, D. (1985). *The interpersonal world of the infant: A view from psychoanalysis and developmental psychology.* New York: Basic Books.

Tannen, D. (1991). *You just don't understand.* New York: William Morrow.

Terr, L. (1990). *Too scared to cry: Psychic trauma in childhood.* New York: Harper & Row.

Terr, L. (1994). *Unchained memories: True stories of traumatic memories, lost and found.* New York: Basic Books.

Udry, J. R. (1988). Biological predispositions and social control in adolescent sexual behaviors. *American Sociological Review, 53*, 709-722.

Udry, J. R., & Billy, J. O. G. (1987). Initiation of coitus in early adolescence. *American Sociological Review, 52*, 841-855.

Udry, J. B., Billy, J. O. G., Morris, N. M., Groff, J. R., & Raj, M. H. (1985). Serum androgenic hormones motivate sexual behavior in adolescent boys. *Fertility and Sterility, 43*, 90-94.

Vander May, B. J. (1988). The sexual victimization of male children: A review of previous research. *Child Abuse and Neglect, 12*, 61-72.

Wang, C. T. & Daro, D. (1995). Current trends in child abuse reporting and fatalities: The results of the 1996 annual fifty-state survey. Chicago: The National Committee to Prevent Child Abuse.

Waites, E. (1993). *Trauma and survival: Post-traumatic and dissociative disorders in women.* New York: Norton.

Webb, N. B. (1991). *Play therapy with children in crisis.* New York: Guilford.

Zaragoza, M. S., Graham, J. R., Hall, G. C. N., Hirschman, R., & Ben-Porath, Y. S. (Eds.). (1995). *Memory and testimony in the child witness.* Thousand Oaks, CA: Sage.

Zivney, O. A., Nash, M. R., & Hulsey, T. L. (1988). Sexual abuse in early versus late childhood: Differing patterns of pathology as revealed on the Rorschach. *Psychotherapy, 25*, 99-106.

Index

About the Authors

Cheryl L. Karp, PhD, is an active member of the American Professional Society on the Abuse of Children (APSAC) and has served as President of the Arizona Chapter. She is also a member of the American Psychological Association. She graduated from the University of Arizona in 1978 and has been in private practice as a licensed psychologist since 1980, specializing in sexual and physical

 abuse issues and forensic psychology, with a clinical emphasis on the effects of trauma. She is the past Clinical Director of the now defunct Trauma Program at Desert Hills Center for Youth and Families, a youth psychiatric hospital and residential treatment center, in Tucson, Arizona. She has coauthored two books, *Treatment Strategies for Abused Children: From Victim to Survivor* (1996), with Traci Butler; and a book with her attorney husband, Leonard Karp, *Domestic Torts: Fam-*

ily Violence, Conflict and Sexual Abuse (Clark Boardman Callaghan, 1989, Supp. 1996). She serves on the editorial board of *Divorce Litigation* and speaks and writes on the subject of domestic torts, battered woman syndrome, child abuse, post-traumatic stress, and the psychologist as expert in forensic cases. She has consulted to the FBI, the U.S. Attorney's Office, Child Protective Services, the Department of Public Safety, and the Department of Corrections.

 **Traci L. Butler, MA,** received her MA from the University of Arizona in counseling and guidance in 1989 and is a national certified counselor. She is currently in private practice and is a school counselor for the Tucson Unified School District. Before this, she was employed as a family therapist and Assistant Director of the Early Childhood Program at Desert Hills Center for Youth and Families in Tucson, Arizona. This program specialized in providing early prevention and intervention for children aged 2 through 11. She has coauthored a book, *Treatment Strategies for Abused Children: From Victim to Survivor* (1996), with Cheryl L. Karp. This book focuses on children aged 6 to 12 who have suffered the effects of childhood abuse. For 5 years, she was a special educator working with children who were experiencing severe emotional difficulties. In addition to her work in the Early Childhood Program, she was a consultant to a residential treatment facility for women substance abusers and their children. She continues to facilitate groups for teenage mothers and fathers to assist them in developing parenting skills. She has presented at workshops and conferences on the issues of child abuse and parenting.

Sage C. Bergstrom, MSW, CISW, is the Clinical Coordinator of the Girls' Residential and Acute Hospital Programs at Desert Hills Center for Youth and Families, a psychiatric facility for children and adolescents in Tucson, Arizona. She is the past Coordinator/ Specialist for the Trauma Recovery Program at that same facility,

 having developed the program with Cheryl L. Karp. She is a graduate of San Francisco State University (1979) and has been in private practice as a psychotherapist since 1981. She specializes in the clinical assessment and psychotherapy of children, adolescents, and adults suffering from emotional, sexual, and physical trauma, as well as in the training of therapists and other caregivers who work with survivors. Most recently, her special clinical interests have been dissociative amnesia, neonaticide, and the vicarious traumatization of caregivers. She has begun working on a doctorate in psychology.

She coauthored the book *A Teacher's Guide to Homosexuality* (1983) and coedited the anthology *Their Special Lives, Their Special Needs: Counseling Lesbian and Gay Youth* (1980). She has served on the teaching faculty of Arizona State University's Graduate School of Social Work and on the counseling faculty of City College of San Francisco. She was also the Coordinator of Counseling Services for a K-8 school district, developing and implementing a range of programs for both students and faculty. She is a member of the American Professional Society on the Abuse of Children (APSAC) and of the National Association of Social Workers (NASW).